SIMON & SCHUSTER

New York   London   Toronto   Sydney   New Delhi

LOUDMOUTH

Tales (and Fantasies) of Sports, Sex, and Salvation from Behind the Microphone

CRAIG CARTON

Simon & Schuster
1230 Avenue of the Americas
New York, NY 10020

First Simon & Schuster hardcover edition June 2013

SIMON & SCHUSTER and colophon are
registered trademarks of Simon & Schuster, Inc.

For information about special discounts for bulk purchases,
please contact Simon & Schuster Special Sales at
1-866-506-1949 or business@simonandschuster.com.

The Simon & Schuster Speakers Bureau can bring authors to your live event.
For more information or to book an event contact the
Simon & Schuster Speakers Bureau at 1-866-248-3049
or visit our website at www.simonspeakers.com.

Designed by Ruth Lee-Mui

Manufactured in the United States of America

1   3   5   7   9   10   8   6   4   2

Library of Congress Cataloging-in-Publication Data

Carton, Craig
Loudmouth: tales (and fantasies) of sports, sex, and salvation from behind the microphone /
Craig Carton.
pages   cm.
1. Carton, Craig, 1969– 2. Sportscasters—New York (State)—Biography. I. Title.
GV742.42.C385C37 2013
070.4'497960922—dc23
[B]   2012048568

ISBN 978-1-4516-4570-5
ISBN 978-1-4516-4574-3 (ebook)

CONTENTS

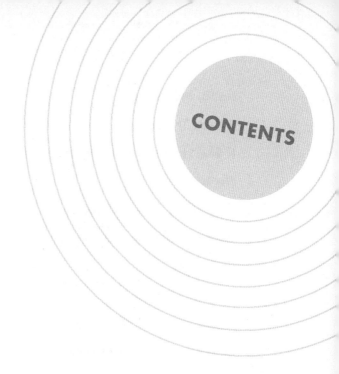

Contents

LOUDMOUTH

I'm all alone in the back of an SUV. It's 35 degrees outside, where there are several thousand people all chanting my name, all wanting to see the clown who for the second year in a row is about to walk across the Brooklyn Bridge in little more than a Speedo and a football jersey.

How did I get myself into this position again, and why in the world does it make me so happy?

It's 10:40 in the morning, and a radio station employee charged with protecting me cracks open the door and asks if I am ready to go. Actually, "ready to do this" are his words.

Not yet.

I take off my sweatpants, revealing my green New York Jets Speedo. Suddenly I have an attack of ego. How's it look? I wonder. I'm not thinking about my legs; I am worried about whether or not my junk looks okay.

"Craigie, Craigie, Craigie!"

The people are restless and cold, too. They want to start the walk. The crowd includes marching bands, mascots, strippers, and thousands of die-hard Jets fans pumped to celebrate their team making it into the AFC Championship game. Holy shit, it's only been eighteen months since I started hosting the *Boomer & Carton* show on WFAN, and now there are thousands of people waiting for me to appear like I'm Phil, the groundhog.

Thankfully I find a pair of ankle socks in my bag and decide to stuff my Speedos with them. It looks so ridiculous, you might think I have hemorrhoids, but I don't care. So I leave them in there; better this way than reality on this cold day.

I take a few more deep breaths and catch my reflection in the rear-view mirror. I freeze. Only one thought, and it's clear.

This is fucking awesome!!!

I swing the door open wide and let the circus begin. The crowd is everything I had hoped it would be. Brooklyn's Cadman Plaza over-flows with all sorts of people: young kids, old men and women, even some people in their Speedos to support me and the Jets—probably more the Jets than me, but they're here. Every local news station is on hand, as are two marching bands and the New York City Police Department, in force. The plan is to walk across the entire span of the Brooklyn Bridge, stopping only at the midway point to do a Jets cheer.

The first face I see when I get out of the SUV is my radio partner's: Boomer Esiason. Boomer was once an NFL MVP for the Cincinnati Bengals, won the Walter Payton Award for Man of the Year, and raised more than $80 million to fight cystic fibrosis. Now he is standing next to his half-naked radio partner and participating in a walk across the bridge with thousands of people whom he would never, under normal circumstances, allow inside his house to use the bathroom. And that's why I love him, and why our show works. Boomer bought in 100 percent to what I thought we had to do to be successful, to get attention, and to connect with a rabid fan base. This bridge walk trumped the Ickey Shuffle by a long shot.

Boomer was on the phone back to the radio station doing a live segment with the midday show on WFAN with Joe Benigno and Evan Roberts. I'm sure those two guys hated having to go to Boomer live for the walk, and I'm even more sure they hated the whole idea of what we were doing. They are straight sports guys, so anything other than a dialogue about the most recent game was outside of their scope of conversation. Plus, Joe had gone out of his way to be an asshole to us when we first started, so having to give us this kind of attention had to kill him—just as Boomer and Carton becoming the number-one-rated show on the station and in morning drive in New York had to bother him to his core.

When we first got to the station, our show, which was the same as it is today, was so different from anything else WFAN had on the air. We replaced Don Imus, who'd been kicked off the air for his "nappy-headed hos" comment, and as a result of replacing Imus and for no other reason, we were deemed lesser talents than him by our fellow hosts. Joe decided it would be a good idea to go on the highly rated afternoon show and attack me by telling their audience that he didn't like me or our show.

I was pissed. Why would Joe, or anybody else for that matter, attack the new morning show? We are his lead-in. The better we do, the better chance he has of getting ratings. His attack made no sense to me. I listened to his comments a few times and then decided I would fight back. Joe attacked because he thought he would ingratiate himself to Mike Francesa, the longtime afternoon show host who also, by his own admission, went out of his way to try to prevent us from being successful.

In reality, Mike didn't give a shit what Joe thought, but he certainly cared about how the station was reacting to us and to this event. So much so that when I called Mike on his behavior years later, he admitted, and I quote: "We were jealous of all the attention you guys were getting." I was later told that as the WFAN newsroom listened to coverage of my walk, Mike came out of his office looking for the info on a story he wanted to talk about on the air later that day. When he couldn't get anyone to turn away, he yelled, "Stop paying attention to some idiot walking across a bridge! I need a sound bite now!"

I had been in radio for nearly twenty years at this point and had been through my share of battles. Joe Benigno wasn't going to attack me on the air and not be told how stupid it was. The next day I started attacking his age, his sound, and his show. He came into the studio where our producer sits, and probably was figuring I would bring him on the air and give him a chance to defend himself, but I gave him no such shot. I waited until we went to a commercial and then called him in.

Before the door could close all the way, I explained in very clear terms how ridiculous and offensive his baseless attack was and that we wouldn't tolerate it again. Joe left the studio without saying a word.

Five years later, our relationship is more than cordial—although we are not friends—and I firmly believe the Joe and Evan midday radio show is the best midday show the radio station has ever had.

• • •

"Craigie is out of the car, and will begin the walk after five strikes of the triangle," Boomer told the WFAN audience. When I was a high school sophomore, my parents made me join the New Rochelle High School Marching Band. I played the drums, but also at one point I had to play the triangle for a particular song. This fact made great fodder for our show, and I felt it only appropriate to relive those days. So out came the triangle, and five hits later, I was on my way.

There is something surreal about having people watch you walk. I not only became aware of how I walked, I became insecure about it. Do I walk funny? Do I have a cool, confident walk? Do I . . . ugh, stop! My brain was in overload. So I stopped walking, raised my bullhorn above my head, and chanted "J-E-T-S! Jets, Jets, Jets!" Luckily, the thousands of people behind me echoed my chant in broken unison. A simple chant, and I was back on my way. God, do I love Jets fans.

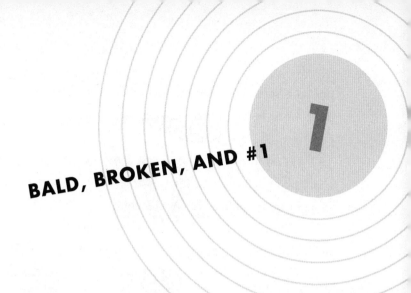

Six-oh-three— nice job, Eddie! Welcome, welcome, welcome! Boomer Esiason and Craig Carton ohhhhhhhhhnnnn The Fan, and we have a great show for you today.

The first time I said that line was on September 4, 2007. It was the single most rewarding professional sentence I've ever spoken. I have been blessed to say it every day now for five years in a row. Some said I would be an "overnight success"; others said I'd never make it. "What a terrible choice," the columnists wrote. "The show has no chance," bloggers predicted. And some listeners complained that I was arrogant and full of myself. I not only remember every negative word written, spoken, and blogged about that first show, I remember every single person who said each thing. I use them and their comments as fuel to drive me to be the best, most successful radio host in the world.

Overnight success, huh?

I was an intern at WFAN Radio twenty-four years ago when they celebrated their first birthday—at a time when most radio experts thought they would never see a second.

"He'll never make it"—okay, asshole, perhaps you forgot to check my background. I was mentored by the legendary Bob Wolfe, the man who called Don Larsen's perfect game in the 1956 World Series, when I took a class at Pace University while still enrolled in high school. Maybe you didn't realize that I was a major ratings success in Buffalo, Cleveland, Philadelphia, and Denver. "What a terrible choice," they said—but did they know that I was the single most-listened-to afternoon radio host in America, or that I was the host around whom an entire syndication company started, which would be heard in more than forty cities?

I was, and am, confident—but hardly cocky or full of myself. Not when I grew up with parents who never fostered self-confidence, but instead locked me in traction to try to knock the Tourette's out of me, or kicked me off the varsity sports teams in high school so I could spend more time studying and join the marching band. My parents were so involved in my life that I was guarded more viciously than the gold at Fort Knox.

I laugh at all of it now. All of the skeptics who said I would never amount to anything in radio. I laugh at the way I was raised. I laugh on the outside, and I put on a good show. Life is like day camp to me. That's my personal mantra, and I try to live up to it as much as I can. But on the inside, I'm still a somewhat insecure child who worries about ratings, about when my show will come to an end, and about not being good enough for my boss, my partner, my wife, and my family.

I can't believe that I host the most-listened-to morning radio show in all of New York, even though I know I'm good enough to do it. I can't believe that I replaced Don Imus and, along with my partner Boomer Esiason, have better ratings every month than Imus had in more than twenty years on the radio. Yet I also believe that there was nobody better in America to replace him than me.

Deep down, I am conflicted. I can't have a basic one-on-one conversation without getting fidgety and uncomfortable, yet I can stand on a stage with a microphone in my hands and perform in front of thousands of people without breaking a sweat or raising my heartbeat. Radio is my salvation; it's my escape from reality. On air, I can be anyone I want to be, and I have chosen to be a super self-confident, fun-loving guys' guy. Off the air, I'm an introverted loner who has no problem staying in the house or avoiding interaction with people. Radio is my drug. I need a microphone and an audience, even if I can't see them, to release my demons—both real and imagined. It's no wonder I picked the most insecure profession in the world to be my life's calling.

Sports and radio: what a wonderful combination. As a kid, the field or the court was my salvation, or my release from reality. From sunup to sundown I was outside playing. As an adult, I did what came most naturally, which was to keep sports in my life by talking about them. The more I get to talk about other people, the less I have to focus on myself. I therefore rarely take days off.

For five years now, the *Boomer & Carton* radio show has been number one in the ratings, and yet I still sweat out my Monday noon phone call with Mark Chernoff, my boss, when he tells me the weekly ratings. I sweat tenths of a point. I get depressed if our lead dwindles by even a fraction of a point, and then celebrate being number one, moments later.

I host the number-one show in radio, and yet my greatest professional satisfaction is being able to tell the naysayers to fuck off. Proving people wrong is a side job for me.

Yet I live every day as if it can all end tomorrow. That being said, when the haters continue to write malicious things about me, one fact cannot be denied: I may be bald and broken, but I made it to the top.

VIETNAM BABY ACT

2

My first and earliest childhood memory is of when I was five years old and attending a Montessori nursery school. Dressed in bad plaids and corduroy, I had to go to the bathroom in the worst way: kidneys ready to explode, legs crossed, hoping to hold back the flow. Meanwhile Joey was in the bathroom and apparently not coming out anytime soon. I held on to a huge wooden block the size of a redwood stump with the bathroom key attached. Finally I couldn't hold it anymore. I pulled my corduroys down to my ankles and started to pee into the small plant the class was raising in hope of relocating it outside.

You would think the real trouble would begin when the teacher caught me doing it. But since it was the end of the day, she didn't say a word. Instead, she beckoned to my mother, who was waiting to take

me home, and brought her into the classroom. My teacher whispered in her ear and set off a whirlwind of trouble for me that would be a constant throughout my life. My mother grabbed me and asked me what I did.

I didn't say anything.

"Did you go number one in that plant?" she asked, more a statement than a question. Again I didn't say anything; already I was exhibiting the traits of a great mob witness. But then I heard the line that still echoes in my ears to this day:

"Wait till your father finds out what you did! You're in big trouble, mister."

When I got home, I wasn't allowed out of my bedroom, as punishment for peeing in the plant. What was I supposed to have done? Wet my pants? Even now, as I look back on it, I think I did the right thing. When my father got home, my mother apprised him of the situation, and he berated me for a while. I don't remember all the specifics, but I do remember what he said right before he left my room: "You will not embarrass us again!"

Wrong, sir. I was just getting started.

Later that summer, my parents decided to enroll me in a local day camp to get me out of the house. The camp was a few miles from our house, and it was typical in that you got to swim, play some sports or do outdoor activities, and then get picked up. It's funny how your brain works, because I have only one memory of that time, and it's got nothing at all to do with the camp itself.

Our neighborhood was filled with kids, and across the street from me lived a kid I will call Frankie Wegurd. Frankie was the only kid I knew who had a Jacuzzi, so we played at his place a lot. Frankie had another thing no one else at the time had, or at least that I knew about: his parents and their best friends swapped spouses.

As the story went, they were swingers who liked to experiment sexually. One night while in that very Jacuzzi, they started fooling around with the opposite spouses. Things heated up, and afterward they got to talking about how they would like to switch partners for a while. As they played out the fantasy, they also realized that they were better matches with each other's spouse. They agreed to separate on a temporary basis and give it a whirl. Frankie's father moved out, and the husband of the other couple moved in. They were divorced and remarried all within a year, and as far as I know, they have stayed that way.

Frankie and I did have one thing in common: we both had dogs. Mine was an old wire-haired terrier that my parents got long before I was born. His name was Tober because he was born in the month of October. One day, Frankie's dog got out of his backyard and came over to our house to play with Tober. They started to growl at each other, and I went to grab Tober's chain to pull him away.

In a split second, Frankie's dog chomped down on my hand. Its teeth punctured my skin below the thumb and scratched my wrist. Frankie yelled louder than anyone I've ever heard before. I was kind of stunned. I didn't yell or cry. I was just in this weird, surreal place, taking it all in. My parents ran outside and saw me bleeding and the dogs barking at each other. They scolded Frankie and his dog, then rushed me to the doctor for a tetanus shot.

It could have been a lot worse, but my parents were furious at Frankie. For a while they forbade him from coming over, because they figured it had to be his fault—as if he had commanded his dog to attack me.

The next day was a camp day, and I remember that I had to decide whether or not I wanted to go, since my hand was bandaged. I'll never forget my mother making me bacon and eggs and my father sitting me on his lap, wearing his typical white T-shirt and jeans. I also remember that my mother liked to save the oil in the pan after cooking the bacon. She would pour the leftover oil into a mason jar and keep it under the kitchen sink, reusing it to cook other meals, or pouring it onto the dog's food. That Tober didn't die of clogged arteries is a minor miracle.

I was gazing out the kitchen window with my brother, waiting for the bus to pick us up, when my father said that he had a rare day off. If I wanted, I could stay home and spend the whole day with him. My father never had a weekday off, and he never wanted to spend his spare time with me. But at this moment life was still good; I hadn't figured out many of the things I would later realize about my parents. I should have said, "Dad, I'm with you; let's go have fun." Instead I said, "No thanks, I want to go to camp."

My father asked me several more times if I was sure I didn't want to hang out with him. I felt guilty over it at the time. We never got to hang out alone, and I was saying no to the opportunity. But instead I decided to go to camp and play. I still regret not saying yes. Who knows what would have happened had I stayed home. I might have had one awesome experience of bonding with my dad. Instead I don't have any memories of that—not to say they're all bad, but I just don't have a single shining one that stands out.

I know my decision stung my father, and I know it for a fact because of what happened a few days later. We were all hanging out in the backyard, and my brother and sister were playing on our big swing. At that point I looked like I could be of Far Eastern descent. I had a round face, almond-shaped eyes, and pin-straight, almost-black hair. My mother had nicknamed me "Bagel" because my face was perfectly round. "If you had a hole in the middle of your face, you would look just like a bagel," she often said. My brother and sister used to tell me that I was adopted from Vietnam. They'd make airplane noises, as if I were landing in America to be adopted, to piss me off. The first Saturday after I decided to go to camp, my father got in on the act.

As my brother and sister made the jet noises, my father cupped his hands over his mouth and pretended to be an airport announcer. "Now arriving from Vietnam on flight 986, little baby boy Carton; let's call him Craig." On and on this taunting went, with my brother and sister making the same sounds as they were swinging and my dad announcing my arrival. After a while I got pissed and yelled at him to stop. I didn't realize that I had walked right in front of the swing, and its corner struck me on the edge of my left eye and sent me flying.

My father's initial reaction wasn't "Oh my God, are you okay?" It was "What the fuck were you walking in front of a swing for, you idiot?"

I got the proper medical attention and a scar above my eye to show for my petulance.

One month later, they were all at it again with the Vietnam baby act. Unbelievably, I walked in front of the same swing and took it in the other eye. And yet again I was scolded for being an idiot. I still have a scar above each eye, but far more important was the realization that I was really on my own, even when surrounded by the people who loved me the most—or the most they were capable of.

THE TOP'S BETTER THAN THE BOTTOM

3

Two recurring dreams were constants throughout my childhood. I had these two dreams when I slipped into bed. I looked forward to them as a way to put the day's distractions aside and allow myself to fall asleep. The first was before I turned ten, and I still smile every time I think about it: I was an undercover FBI agent passing myself off as an elementary school student. I gave myself superpowers, such as creating the world's first invisible water slide that could carry me to any part of the school. As bad guys invaded the playground, I turned invisible, too.

The second one was far beyond my maturity level. I dreamed that one day I would be famous enough to appear on the Johnny Carson show. Not only was I a guest, I had something specific to say. What did I desperately need to tell the world? My message was as simple as

it was important for me at that time: in my dream, I wanted to tell the world that my father was a disciplinarian; that life wasn't fun growing up inside the walls of the Carton family prison. And yet if not for the way my parents raised me, I wouldn't have gotten to the places I had.

I was one fucked-up kid.

The desire to be famous lived in my subconscious. I never contemplated it when I was awake. But uttering those words about my family life motivated me and gave me a sense of peace.

To be clear, I don't hate my father. I love him, and I spent a good portion of my life trying to please him. Yet I also find it hard to spend time with him, and at this point I don't care in the least what he thinks of me or how I live my life.

My father grew up throughout the five boroughs of New York City, and he grew up tough. He had no choice. His father, Jack Carton, was one of the toughest guys in New York in the 1930s. A Golden Gloves champion twice as a middleweight, a standout lifeguard on the beaches of Coney Island, an accomplished pilot, and the muscle for the Jewish mob, nobody fucked with my grandfather.

Nobody, that is, except cancer.

By all accounts, what Jack Carton said, went. After a stint in the army, where he taught soldiers how to fly the latest military planes, he opened up a gas station and diner on Flatbush Avenue in Brooklyn. When he fought for the Golden Gloves, the *Post* accidentally printed his name as Jack *Carter*. Attempting to capitalize on the notoriety, he called his diner Carter's and used the tagline "Good to the Last Morsel." He worked eighteen-hour days to support his family, which consisted of my father, my aunt Meryl, and my grandmother.

Jack believed in the handshake over the hug, that a man should act like a man, and not reveal his emotions. He didn't spend much time with his kids, but he noticed that my dad was starting to make some bad choices—such as joining a gang—so he decided to teach him a lesson. He told my father that he, my dad, was going to work side by side with him for the whole summer, doing manual labor from sunup to sundown for ten weeks straight. At the end of the summer, Jack sat my dad down and said, "Son, you have a choice in life. You can earn a living with your hands like you just experienced, or with your brain. It's a decision you have to make."

My father chose to live by his brains and wound up excelling at school, being voted class president, and enrolling at Alfred University. My grandfather never saw him graduate. He died of leukemia when my dad was a sophomore in college. My dad could have dropped out, but he decided to honor his father by graduating. Unfortunately, my father also decided to inherit many of his dad's traits.

My mother, Bobbe, was born Roberta Louise Rosen to a poor family in New Jersey and spent a few years as a child in South Carolina before moving back to Whippany, New Jersey. Her father was a brilliant engineer who wound up getting work at the Newark, New Jersey, airline hangars in between World Wars I and II. When work dried up there, he became a door-to-door salesman, selling whatever products he could. My grandmother never worked a day in her life. From what I've been told, she was borderline loopy, and as my mother describes it, her loopiness led her to wild swings of emotion, and she was cold and quiet, although she was never medicated or hospitalized. For my mother, every day could be bad.

As a kid, my mother excelled academically, and her high school grades were so good that she was offered one of the first-ever full academic scholarships handed out at Johns Hopkins University. But she never went. My grandparents decided that it was too expensive even to drive her there, to Baltimore, and that their money would be better spent sending her brother to college instead. It was a man's world, they reasoned, and they made this decision without considering how it affected my mother.

The next summer, my mother did some summer stock theater, which resulted in her being nicknamed Chesty Larue. I don't know that she ever danced or shook her ass for money, or if "Chesty" was merely a character she played in a show, but ever since I first heard the nickname, I have teased her about it. The following fall, my mother went to nursing school. She became a registered nurse and worked at Mount Sinai Hospital, where she met my father. I have always admired her for overcoming her parents' not thinking she was good enough. She became a real estate broker and agent in her thirties, and owned her own successful real estate agency in New Rochelle, New York, for more than a decade before retiring. Sadly, though, she inherited her parents' knack for being emotionless and inconsiderate when it came to decisions that affected their kids.

I grew up without hugs, kisses, or verbal confirmation of being loved. It was all I knew, and I accepted it for what it was well into my adult life. At that point, I began to resent my father for not being warmer toward me. But the resentment morphed into feeling sorry for my dad and forgiving him. That was the only way he knew to act. I once asked him why he was so cynical, and when he got that way. He replied, "When I was eighteen." He didn't have to elaborate; that was when his father died from cancer.

I think about my dad a lot, yet I don't see him or talk to him much now; certainly not as often as when I used to call him daily just to stay in touch. I view him as a cautionary example that drives me to love my children and make sure they know it, feel it, and hear me say it often. I try hard to do better than he did. And yet I also hope I'm as successful a parent as he was. He raised three kids who are doing amazingly well today, regardless of whether it's in spite of him or because of him.

What kind of asshole am I that I would say that, and would still think about my childish desire to tell the world that I didn't like living with my parents? Well, that's the thing about me: I look at life through the split prism of a forty-year-old man and a ten-year-old child. I am both immature and mature at the same time. I filled out an application to join the FBI when I was in my mid-twenties and living in Philadelphia, only to realize that there were no invisible water slides to transport me to the scene of a crime. I never sent in my application.

To me, life should be like day camp. Yet I have to make adult decisions that impact my wife, my kids, my work partners, and so many others. I'm always happy—that's what they say about me, and that's what I say about myself—but I can't say I know what happiness is, other than whenever I look at my wife and kids.

One aspect of my mental well-being, or lack thereof, is that I have been diagnosed with multiple disorders: Tourette's, OCD, ADD—I have them all. They drive every movement I make and every thought that enters my mind. Everything has to be done in even numbers. If I touch something twice with my left hand, I have to touch it twice with my right. I have to take an even number of steps before I hit a crack in the sidewalk. When I golf, I can't swing a club unless I take an odd number of practice swings, so the real swing winds up on an even number.

The OCD is relentless, yet it combats my lack of focus from the ADD. Most of the time the OCD wins because the Tourette's comes into play. When I have a Tourette's tic, such as having to touch my nose and sniffle, it has to be done in a specific way, or my brain will not allow me to move on. If I do not tic in a precise manner, I may as well be locked in mental prison, as I can't do anything without performing the tic "right."

When I was living in Denver, my wife, Kim, at the time still my girlfriend, came to visit. We were at a red light in the car, and I had to tic. As an adult, I've become good at hiding these physical urges so you'd never know I had any. But this time I couldn't hold it back. I put my right hand to my face and started to do a combination of touches and taps to my nose and face while sniffling in an uncontrollable manner. I couldn't get it just right, or in the perfect order. The traffic light turned green, but I was locked inside the Tourette's. The light turned red, and we still hadn't moved. Finally I performed the motions in the appropriate manner to release the lock on my brain. I looked at Kim and she said, "What the fuck was that?"

"I have Tourette's. Let's go grab dinner."

I'm in a constant battle with myself, and I've survived it without ever telling a soul—until now. I built a career based on one lousy college demo tape. I suffered the indignity of being fired without cause. I never had a single girlfriend for more than three weeks, and yet I married the best-looking girl I ever dated, who came with a unique personality to match. I never played professional baseball, but several dozen strippers and Hooters girls will swear to their kids that they slept with the backup third baseman of the Philadelphia Phillies.

I've been to the bottom career-wise, and now I am blessed to have been to the top. The top is much better than the bottom—unless, of course, you're a veteran porn actor who likes that sort of thing.

A GOOD DOSE OF SCANDAL 4

There's an old cliché that nothing is certain but death and taxes. While that might be true (unless you are Ted Williams's head or Wesley Snipes's accountant), the truism is off the mark. The only thing that is for certain is that no matter what anyone says or thinks, every good story that has ever been told includes a scandal.

Scandal is the air we breathe, the gravity that keeps us grounded, the m.o. in our mojo—well, you get it.

Scandal has evolved, or perhaps *de*volved, ever since the original debate over how the earth was formed. Do you really believe that there was an explosion in mid-space, and we got lucky enough that five billion years later Brooklyn Decker was born and, even more amazingly, agreed to sleep with a perennial loser like Andy Roddick for the rest of her life? Or maybe you believe that there is a higher being who decided one day that he needed a planet to play with, so in six days he created the earth, and was so satisfied with his work that he took Sunday off? When he got back to work, humans could have started our existence with the wheel, or the ability to make fire—or the ability of a 120-pound, slightly built American with no muscle mass to speak of to ride his bike through the Alps without putting some type of cancer-causing poison into his blood.

Regardless of what you believe, scandal has indeed devolved into one of three areas, and every single controversy can be traced back to one of them. The Big Three, as I call them, are:

SEX, DRUGS, and CHEATING.

Two of the biggest cheating scandals happened nearly one hundred years apart. The first and probably most famous was the 1919 Black Sox scandal. Orchestrated by the notorious Arnold "the Brain" Rothstein, it involved several members of the Chicago White Sox conspiring with gamblers to intentionally lose the World Series. As a result, eight members of the White Sox organization, including superstar "Shoeless" Joe Jackson, were banned from Major League Baseball.

The second was the Tim Donaghy scandal in 2007. Donaghy was a thirteen-year veteran official in the NBA. He had a big gambling habit, which resulted in him owing lots of money to the mob. He saw only one way out of the debt: placing thousands of dollars in bets on games that he was officiating. As a ref, he could control the final score by either blowing or not blowing his whistle in certain situations. Tim also provided mobsters with tips on who would win. The guilty verdict was a major blow to the credibility of the NBA, which continues to fight the appearance of impropriety with every playoff.

The biggest drug scandals in sports involved steroid use or other types of performance-enhancing drugs. There was a time when drug scandals meant your favorite player got caught snorting a line of cocaine off a stripper's ass, or simply that he played for the Dallas Cowboys in the 1990s—but not anymore.

Today's top drug scandals involve every sport, both amateur and pro. In baseball, it's Barry Bonds, the all-time lead home run hitter, and Roger Clemens, the all-time Cy Young Award winner. Both linked to steroids; both the best at what they did; and both most likely never going into the Hall of Fame. And let's not forget that Lance Armstrong, the most dedicated cyclist in the history of two wheels, recently admitted to years of blood doping throughout his storied career. In an interview with Oprah Winfrey, he claimed to have cheated during every one of his seven Tour de France wins. He said that he never thought of it as cheating because he figured everyone else was doing it. I tried that line of thinking once with my parents when I told them everyone else was getting high, but it didn't seem to work.

The biggest sex scandal of all time would have to be Tiger Woods banging half of North America while married. The most amazing part of Tiger's cheating is that he won more major golf tournaments than any golfer playing on the tour, all the while juggling a wife, two kids, more than a dozen other women on multiple continents, and all the other shit that he must have had to do on a daily basis. This guy won more majors than any dude since Jack Nicklaus.

This proves my point that golf is the world's single most boring sport. He was so bored that in between shots, he had to spend his time setting up liaisons for after the round. And now that he's divorced and apparently not banging half the free world, his golf game has gone to shit.

There is no area more rife with scandal than the world of sports. Politics is right up there, but I'm not Bill O'Reilly, so for this book we will focus on scandals that helped shape sports.

For a guy like me, scandal is good business. Hell, for all of us, scandal is good business. Without scandal, what would millions of housewives have to talk about with each other; what would bartenders and their regulars chat about? Without scandal, we'd be reduced to talking about the weather.

My first introduction to scandal took place when I was eight years old and playing youth soccer in New Rochelle, just north of the Bronx. My team had advanced to the championship game. I was the star player on the team. (Did you think I'd tell a story where I wasn't the star?)

This, though, is the true story of a boy and his soccer ball—and his Benedict Arnold of a mother. At these events, the parents kept the official clock, and many would arbitrarily extend the length of a game if their kid's team was losing. Conversely, some parents shortened games to preserve one-goal leads, so their little future non-athletes could win.

By the time we had made it to the championship, the league decided something had to be done, so they searched high and low for the fairest maiden of them all to keep the official clock. They chose my mother. Big-chested, yes; fair, fuck no! Not once could I eat a Drake's Ring Ding if I didn't shove broccoli down my gullet first. This woman wouldn't let me go trick-or-treating one Halloween because I had a test two days later. My mother might have been a former burlesque dancer named Chesty Larue, but now she was the most honest gal in the neighborhood? Laughable!

I told her to keep it fair and gave her a wink. She didn't react. I guess I should have put a couple of singles in her G-string. As the game continued, a terrible rainstorm overtook us and we played in a torrential downpour. Scoreless at halftime with thirty minutes to go . . . We were playing in mud up to our ankles, and the prospects of scoring grew smaller as the afternoon grew older. No way would they cancel the game and require parents to give up another Sunday to watch their spoiled kids run around on a field—not when it cut into "parental alone time," as my folks called it. (I think we call it "fucking" now, but I'm not sure. My wife and I call it "Mommy and Daddy conversation time," but we haven't said a word to each other privately without fucking in years.)

Regulation came and went, and still scoreless. To overtime we went.

Five minutes one way, and still tied.

Five minutes the other way, and still tied.

Sudden death it would be.

Five more minutes one way, and still tied.

Five more sudden-death minutes the other way; still tied.

The parents convened and decided they would pull the goalies and play more sudden death.

Five minutes more, and we were still tied.

Five more scoreless minutes, and unbelievably, we were still tied.

They put the goalies back in, but took a position player off the field so there would be more room to run and make a play.

Five minutes like that, and still tied.

An epic game for the ages.

As the clock ticked down in the umpteenth overtime session, I moved the ball from my right foot to my left and got by a defender on the left wing. I came back to the right foot about thirty yards away from the goal and, rain pounding my body, I stepped into the mud, four seconds remaining. I came down hard and made contact with the ball at three seconds left. The ball headed toward the goal—two seconds— the goalie dove, but the ball was out of his reach. One second. The ball sailed into the net's upper right-hand corner; it's a game-winning goal, smack-dab at zero seconds—game over, we won! My father ran onto the field and knocked me to the ground, then picked me up and put me on his shoulders. His son had just scored the greatest goal in the history of youth soccer. We were going to celebrate, goddamn it.

Parents from the other team stormed the field and made a beeline for the referee. They surrounded him, yelling and pushing, demanding to know if the clock ran out before or after the ball went into the net. They all turned as one and looked at my mother, who had the timer in her hands. It was up to the former summer stock dancer to decide our fate. She alone would choose whether or not I would have the greatest memory any kid could ever have and go on to play in the state tournament, or take the victory away from me. Knowing that the other parents had cheated the clock many times, she drew herself up, conscious of everyone awaiting her verdict, and pronounced: "The clock hit zero before it went into the net"—stabbing her own son in the back.

Tie game, pandemonium, too much mayhem to restore order. As a result, we had to replay the whole thing the following week. Score: 3–1, their favor.

How could she do that to me? How about one for the home team, Mom? As the crowd of parents grew more aggressive, I heard shouts aimed at my mother, from "Don't be a cheater!" to "We know where you live!" to "Do the right thing!" Parents of my teammates thought for sure the goal was scored before the clock ran out, and parents of our opponents thought time must have expired. Whichever way she went, she would be accused of having fixed the score—scandal either way, for sure. Maybe she saw it as a way of gaining importance in the eyes of the other parents—as opposed to being seen as just a broad with a big chest. The game was talked about for years to come, and came to redefine who kept the clock and how it was kept. You'd think it was a World Cup game that had been decided by a referees' call, like the famous or infamous Maradona "Hand of God" goal that propelled Argentina to the 1986 World Cup title.

The soccer game of 1977 defined my relationship with my mother, and still does. It may not have been influenced by the hand of God, but it sure as hell had something to do with the Boobs of Bobbe.

Tim Tebow is the backup quarterback for my beloved New York Jets. Why? I have no idea.

Most people have fallen in love with Tim and the religion that he is so passionate about. I have come to believe that Tebow is sincere, that his whole persona is not an act, and that he believes it to his core. But there is one aspect of the Tebowmania that I refuse to buy. What kind of guy could possibly live the life he proclaims to live when he is surrounded by constant temptation?

First off, having met Tim and had him on my radio show, I can attest that he might be the single most handsome dude I have ever seen up close. I love Mark Sanchez and Alex Rodriguez, and they would win most beauty contests, but this Tebow is on another planet. He's a great athlete—arguably the best college QB ever—and he just so

happened to go to the University of Florida, which has more hot girls on campus per square inch than just about any other school in the country. Yet he professed to be a virgin through his graduation.

Bullshit!

He was drafted by the Denver Broncos and guaranteed millions of dollars.

Still a virgin.

Bullshit!

He leads the Broncos to a whole bunch of last-second wins, and even helps them win a playoff game for the first time in almost a decade.

Still a virgin.

Bullshit!

During that magical run with the Broncos, he has a cold sore on his lip for a month.

Still a virgin.

Bullshit!

In Tebow's first month with the Jets, his buddy and fellow QB Mark Sanchez is linked to a minimum of three celebrity women, each one hotter than the next. Tebow describes his only meaningful relationship as the one he has with a church advisor who keeps him on the straight and narrow.

Still a virgin.

Okay . . . maybe.

Right before the season begins, *GQ* publishes photos of Tebow with no shirt on, posing as Sexy Jesus. Local New York City television crews catch him running in the rain with his shirt off in front of female fans who are passing out from the sight of his pecs.

Still a virgin.

Bullshit!

Of all the things that my brain cannot process—such as how in the world we can push ten random numeric buttons on a small box and start talking with someone halfway around the world, let alone next door—what tops the list is that a good-looking, successful superstar who has women throwing themselves at him like women used to fling panties at Tom Jones has never, not even once, experienced the nectar of the forbidden fruit.

I can only imagine how his head is going to explode when he does it for the first time. Not only because of how great it is, but because he'll realize how much he's passed on, up until that point.

I hate him now.

Okay . . . bullshit.

CLOCKWORK ORANGE, FOR REAL (OR, HOW I CAME TO LOVE BASEBALL)

Imagine being locked in a room against your will.

Really locked, and not in a room that you could move around in. I mean locked in one position for four days.

You cannot move without your captors' help, and even then it's just to go to the bathroom or to eat. While you're lying there, you can have the television on, but you can only pick one thing to watch. What would you choose to see?

But let me step back for a minute and set the scene. The year was 1976 and I was seven years old, a first-grade student in Roosevelt Elementary School on North Avenue in New Rochelle. An old three-story brick building, the school consisted of grades from kindergarten to sixth. I learned my first curse word there, played kickball for the first time, tackled and kissed a girl for the first time, and—maybe my finest memory—got to climb the rope in gym class and feel the sensation of friction against my junk for the first time. Climbing the rope became my single favorite activity in elementary school. I would climb high and slow, and enjoy every minute of it.

Suffice it to say, at that point I was a normal kid, except for one thing. Earlier that year, I had developed a "problem," as my folks put it. I would reach across the dinner table and knock the water pitcher over.

Apparently I did this a lot, and it pissed my parents off. We had a clam-shaped table in our kitchen, which we sat around for meals. My mother always put a big glass pitcher of water on the table for us to share. The pitcher was never near me, it seemed, and it was too big for my brother or sister to pick up. So whenever I wanted to refill my glass, I had to reach across the table to get it.

I frequently knocked it over—not because I meant to, but because it was big and heavy, and I couldn't quite grasp it. You would think someone would fill my glass before dinner and eliminate the problem. But instead the pitcher stayed, I kept knocking it down, and my parents kept yelling at me. They also said I blinked excessively, especially after making a mess with the water.

After several months of wet tables and blinking, and no one thinking they ought to move the pitcher closer to me, my folks decided to send me to the neighborhood shrink. His office was inside his house, and I wondered if the guy was for real. If he was, why didn't he have a real office?

He was a nice enough man, and he took me into his play area to chat while my folks had to wait outside. I liked that they were not allowed in the room with me, but I still didn't know why I was there. Sure, I blinked and spilled the water. I also believed that inanimate objects had feelings—specifically this one large rock that was at the end of our driveway. The rock was huge, too big for three of us kids to budge an inch, and we tried damn near every day. I started to talk to the rock to encourage it to move. One day I painted the rock just to see if he—that's right, the rock had a cock—would like being a different color. That rock never did move, of course, but I spoke to it every day until I was in high school, when I realized that talking to a rock might be considered weird. After that, I decided to communicate with it telepathically, and I did so until the day I went to college. But then again, who didn't believe weird stuff at age seven?

The doctor played cards with me, and then we moved to a mean round of Othello. During the games, he asked me why I kept spilling the water. I told him that I didn't do it on purpose, that it happened because I had to reach all the way across the table. Then he asked why I blinked. I told him I didn't think I blinked more than the average kid. He asked me more questions for half an hour. I didn't give him anything he could use against me, since I was already a seasoned mob witness in my own mind.

Earlier that year, I was coming back to school after lunch at the nearby strip mall with a friend of mine, Max. My friends and I did this every day, as back then the school allowed it. On this particular day, three teenagers approached me and Max in an alleyway, shoved us up against the wall, and demanded any money or jewelry we had. I pushed one of the kids and told Max to run with me. As I sprinted away, Max stayed put, frozen in fear. By the time I realized he wasn't next to me, I was three blocks up the street. I couldn't just leave him there, so I ran to the crossing guard and told her what had happened. When we got to the alley, the kids ran away, leaving Max crying. They stole his necklace and a few bucks. But more than that, they stole his confidence. He didn't go out to lunch again for the rest of the year.

About a week later, on a Saturday morning, New Rochelle police officers came to my house. They had caught the kids who held up Max, and wanted me to testify in court. That was a nonstarter in my family. My father told them it wasn't going to happen, and just like out of the movie A Bronx Tale, the officers bypassed my dad and said, "Son, could you identify the kids that stopped you in the alleyway?"

Of course I could, but now, with my father in front of me, I knew the right answer: "Sorry, officer, I don't think I could." The cop gave me his card so I could call him if I changed my mind; then he left.

Based on this experience, I knew how to avoid giving anything away to the shrink. When he allowed my folks back into the room with us, he told them that I was a normal kid. They disagreed. They wanted something to be wrong with me—not because they wanted their son to be broken, but so they could blame me for the behavior that bugged them.

A few weeks later, I developed a habit of moving my neck around when it was stiff, as if to crack it. One day while walking into the entrance of my school, I went to loosen my neck and I felt a ping. I was sent to the nurse's office because it hurt, and she put a neck brace on me. My mother came to pick me up, and when I got home, I lay down on the couch to see if I'd feel any better.

A few hours later, my dad came home early, which put me on alert because he never left work before six. He was accompanied by a strange man who was carrying a weird contraption with metal bars. For about an hour they worked in my bedroom with the door shut, and then the guy left.

My parents summoned me to my room, where I was shocked to see this huge device with bars and a collar hanging over my bed. My parents told me that they were concerned about the repeated neck-loosening. They wanted to help me stop doing it. I was to lie in bed with my neck immobilized. This device would put an end to my twitching neck.

In other words, forced behavior therapy was about to take place, with me as the guinea pig. Think *Clockwork Orange*, but for real. I was in trouble, but what could I say or do about it? From the grim expressions on their faces, I realized I had no choice.

I put on my pajamas and climbed into bed. My parents fitted the metal collar around me and connected me to the machine. Held motionless, I couldn't move my head, neck, or shoulders even an inch in any direction. They then wheeled in our only television, a nineteen-inch set that had the six channels all New Yorkers got back then, long before the days of ESPN. They even gave me a choice of what I wanted to watch. The remote control hadn't been invented yet, so this would be my only channel for the duration of my lockdown. Fuck!!!

Thank God the day I was locked in that thing, the Major League Game of the Week was on. There was no kid programming back then, but there was baseball, and there was Joe Garagiola. I fell in love with him and baseball that day and have never stopped loving it. I can still close my eyes and hear Joe announce what the Oakland A's were doing. I guess Joe could have been any announcer that day, but his ability just to talk and talk and talk about baseball with such love, admiration, and passion grabbed hold of me and allowed me to daydream away from being locked in traction, and into the ballpark. I just wish I could thank Joe for freeing me.

Since I have Tourette's, the neck twitching and blinking were out of my control, no matter how much my parents thought I did it to annoy them. As for the water spilling, I guess I was just clumsy. I was too young to hate my parents, but I wasn't too young to become fearful of them, which is what I did. Not being loved, or told I was loved, did two profound things to me. First, it created a disconnect between me and my parents, which led me to hide as many things as I could from them and not be open about anything with them—and ultimately with anyone else, either. I figured if I didn't reveal what I was doing or thinking, there was no way they could put me in traction or punish me in other ways. I was already a quiet kid around adults, so this wasn't hard to do. Sure, my parents thought they were helping me. They even invited my relatives to come see the freak boy in the traction machine. Baseball was my savior that week, and I will never forget it.

On the other hand, the Tourette's wasn't as easy to cope with. I didn't know what it was called, but I knew I blinked and twitched. I started to figure out that I could control the tics for a certain length of time, only to have a major explosion later on. And that's what I did. Whenever I was around my parents, I tried to suppress the urge to twitch. When I felt I couldn't anymore, I would try to make sure I was alone in my room or outside where nobody would see. I pulled this off from first grade until I was thirty, and then I got busted.

CONFUCIUS SAY: TRY NOT TO PUKE ON EGG ROLL

6

When I was a kid, I looked forward to Sunday evenings, when we always went to a Chinese restaurant. For one thing, I didn't have to eat my mother's cooking—not that she was a bad cook, but she made the same thing over and over again. How in the world can you fuck up meat loaf when you make it every single week for more than a decade? My mom would routinely go to the mason jar of oil and drop pieces of chicken into what looked like the *Exxon Valdez* spill, again and again and again. And we would eat it, again and again and again.

Sundays were a reprieve from that, although our custom was just as repetitive as with at-home meals. We went to the same restaurant, Szechuan Empire, at the same time, 6 p.m. We always sat at the same table, and had the same waiter named Henry. His real name couldn't

have been Henry, but the restaurant's owner made the Chinese staff take American names that were more pronounceable. The place was full of Johns and Steves and Bobs, none of whom spoke English.

As a boy, my Chinese food regimen was simple: egg roll, spare ribs, dumplings, lo mein—the same shit every time. I would never eat seafood; I just didn't care for it, and I wasn't going to risk trying anything new after my recent fiasco with onion soup. My family had gone out to eat at a steak and chops place, and I saw someone at a nearby table order French onion soup that arrived bubbling over with cheese and a big piece of French bread. It looked so good—like garlic bread with melted mozzarella. I begged my folks to let me order it. After a few minutes of pleading, they relented, with the proviso that I had to finish it so they didn't waste their money. God forbid I didn't like it.

The soup came and looked wonderful. I jumped right into the ooey gooey cheese and bread. I loved it, but then I got to the onion broth underneath. It was disgusting, so I didn't take a second spoonful. My parents yelled at me for wasting their money and told me I had to finish it or there would be no dinner. For a full hour they watched as I tried to sip the soup but never made a dent in it. They held to their word. I was not getting dinner. It was the first, but not the last, time I left a restaurant hungry.

Later the same year, I had the single worst eating experience of my life. A fall Sunday brought about great change to the Cartons' mundane routine. My folks had heard of a new Chinese place opening in a neighboring town, the same week that our beloved Henry was back in China visiting his family. My father decided that it was a good time to cheat on the Empire and try a new restaurant.

Now, my father is not a cheater. He isn't a drinker or a gambler, either. But on this day, he threw caution to the winds and decided to have an affair with another Chinese restaurant. I asked for my usual items, and everything was fine until he ordered the entrees. My dad is a control freak. Nobody else, including my mother, was ever allowed to order. He was the only one who spoke to the waiter. If you wanted something, you had to run it by him. Then, like Judge Judy, he would contemplate the request and make a ruling on it. Typically the answer was "Guilty," or "No!"

I should have known that something bad was going to happen, since viewing Halley's comet was a more common occurrence than Dad changing what we ate. Yet here we were in a new restaurant, and my dad was switching what we ordered. I had finished my egg roll and a spare rib when he announced that tonight was the night I was going to try shrimp.

I'm a father now, and I agree with broadening my kids' horizons and having them experiment with new things. But my dad, who months earlier wouldn't allow me to eat dinner because I had tried something new and didn't like it, was now going to force something on me that I didn't want to eat—in public. It didn't make sense then, and it still doesn't, thirty years later.

The shrimp came, and I started to sweat. He put one on my plate and said I had to try it. I protested: "Dad, I like what I like. I don't want it." We argued back and forth. I wouldn't budge, but neither would he. My mother, brother, and sister sat there helplessly as we battled. This showdown was Rocky versus Apollo Creed, except that he was my father and I wasn't going to win, no matter how much I tried or fought back. I relented, and he shoved the shrimp into my mouth. I gagged and threw up all over the table. I was humiliated and pissed off, but I wasn't the only one. My father thought I did it on purpose to embarrass him. He yelled at me, then pulled me out of the restaurant by my collar, shoved me into the back of our car, told me to wait there while they finished dinner, locked the door, then went back inside.

When they came out forty-five minutes later, he was still fuming at me. "How dare you do that!" I said, "I didn't want the shrimp! You forced it on me. It's not my fault I threw up!" We argued for most of the trip, until he'd had enough. He pulled the car over, kicked me out more than a mile from our house, and told me to walk home. After I got out of the car, he pulled away and never looked back.

When I got to our house, my father was in his room for the night. He didn't want to talk to me. My mother asked if I was okay, and then she went to bed. I brushed my teeth and went to bed, and we have never talked about it again. Nowadays when I go to a restaurant, I order every single thing on the appetizer menu—just because I can.

Growing up, one of the things that distracted me from my problems was listening to the radio. There were only four stations I ever listened to. WCBS-FM was the best oldies station in America. I always identified with oldies because my father loved '50s music, and the songs were catchy and easy to memorize. I must have sung "Chantilly Lace" a million times. Motown also grabbed me at an early age, because I could always identify with the lyrics.

The second station I got turned on to was WNBC, but only for one guy, Howard Stern. Howard talked in a way I had never heard anybody talk before. He was brutally honest and laugh-out-loud funny. I've always felt that he was the best person who ever hosted a talk show, because he was the first and only guy who gave me the feeling that if I turned off his show, I would miss something. This is well before he started doing as much of the sexual content that he became so famous for. He was irreverent, in-your-face, and he was a master at making you hang on to his every word.

I have always felt that people who classify Howard as a guy who only talks about sex or naked girls completely miss the boat. The sexual content is what grabbed most people and got him headlines, for sure, but if you ever stopped to listen to all the other content, which was more than half of his show, you would recognize that Howard was and is brilliant. He is the best interviewer I have ever heard to this day, and he has an amazingly articulate way of making you care about what he says. He has to be the only guy who can make more than fifty million dollars a year and be driven to work in a limo, yet still appeal to the blue-collar guy making fifty grand.

The third station I grew to really like was Z-100 in the heyday of Scott Shannon and the Morning Zoo. I liked the music more than anything, but with Howard still on in the afternoons and no real contemporary of his in the morning, Shannon was the best thing coming out of New York. He also had a very funny character named Mr. Leonard. Listening to these great shows probably stirred the beginnings of my interest in radio, although I didn't even realize it back then. At the time, it was just a way to relax and take my mind off my parents' control-freak ways.

I HATE SUNDAYS

I hate Sundays—always have. I know how ludicrous that sounds since Sunday is a day off with NFL football, and is still a whole day away from Monday. My disgust for the day dates all the way back to when I was a small child in the 1970s. Sunday is the day that always brought the most conflict. The other days are easy:

Monday: Work and get ready for *Monday Night Football.* Hope that the waitress bringing your wings and beer is hot, because your buddies aren't.

Tuesday: Recover from the night before and get through work without being fired for saying something to the sexy new girl at the office.

Wednesday: Week's almost over. Start putting in order which girls you are going to call first for the weekend.

Thursday: Best night out: no amateurs, and the chances are high of meeting a new girl and getting her number for a weekend date.

Friday: Work is out and happy hour is on, and the strippers all know my name.

Saturday: Sleep until noon, start drinking during the SEC Game of the Week, and make sure your jeans are clean so you can wear them again when you go out.

Sunday: Just have to wake up in time for *NFL Today* on CBS, and before my bookie closes up shop for the one o'clock games.

No matter when you wake up on Sunday, you know that the clock is ticking toward Monday morning. At least you can roll out of bed late, sit on the couch, and watch football all day long from September to February—or make it three straight drinking days, watching games at the local tavern with your friends.

Still, at some point, it's going to be nighttime, and you've got to prepare for the buzzing alarm clock. Even so, I look forward to Sunday all week long, especially during football season. But since I was a kid, I also hated the seventh day of the week. Sunday wasn't a day of rest from punishing me or making life miserable for me. Sunday was worse than every other day.

For most Jews born before 1950, religion was important, and understandably so. These adults were children of the Great Depression, and their parents most likely immigrated to this country during or near the time of the Holocaust. Their kids would be raised Jewish.

Although I'm Jewish, I detest and resent religion, and I believe that people who live their lives by the notion that there is a higher being watching and judging us are nuts. There's no proof whatsoever that a higher being exists—any more than there's evidence that we were seeded by aliens. And also, if there *were* a higher power, then why—oh fuck it, there isn't one, as far as I can tell.

While I don't believe in God, I do acknowledge that many of the tenets of religion are powerful ideas—some of which I even agree with.

Thou shalt not kill. That makes sense. Thou shalt not bang thy neighbor's wife. I agree with this one, and if you saw my neighbor's wife, you would, too. You've got to believe that commandment came from a guy with a hot wife and ugly neighbors.

While religion is bad enough, I don't get adults who are born-again. They seem to find religion later in life, and it becomes their entire way of life, and anything less is offensive to them. When you grow up with religion in the house, it's all you know; but it seems to me that these born-agains don't respect anyone who doesn't want to hear the preachings of a fifty-five-year-old who thinks the sun rises and sets on his newfound beliefs.

There is one caveat, and that is the guys or gals who find religion while incarcerated.

My single biggest fear is being locked up in jail. It's irrational, but I think about it often. I have two rules of thumb if I ever do get arrested, and these rules apply to any level of jail—even a holding cell for an hour for a driving ticket.

Rule #1 is to act crazy and start mumbling out loud. The more gibberish, the better. Seems to me that in every movie that includes a jail scene, no one wants to mess with or fuck the crazy guy.

Rule #2: Find religion as quickly as possible. Jail is broken up into gangs, as far as I can tell, and they are based on race and religion. I'm Jewish and white, but if I thought finding Allah would protect my precious rear end, I would buy the Koran, change my name to Muhammad Ali Carton, and start believing.

But short of the above happening, I think I'm going to take my chances being atheist here on the outside.

• • •

Growing up, I resented religion. It was forced upon me as a kid in the form of mandatory Hebrew school every Sunday. I had to attend school six days a week. Regular school was boring enough, but to have to get up early and go to Hebrew school was the worst. I have nothing against the fine people who dedicated their lives to raising us Jewish and explaining Judaism to me, but I hated the program.

The only good thing about Hebrew school was that there was a playground. The hiccup was that you didn't get to have recess. You learned about being Jewish for three hours, and then you went home. I didn't care about learning about the Pharaoh and letting my people go. I read the Ten Commandments once, and I got it. I sang the same songs every Passover, I lit the eight candles every Hanukkah—what more did I need to know?

So in between classes, I would invariably find my way outside to the playground. Each time I did, a teacher came to get me. A note was always sent home. The first few times I threw the note out, but when I didn't bring it back signed or my parents didn't call the school as requested, the teacher called my folks to let them know that I was a miscreant.

What always surprised me was that I could rarely get my friends to go outside with me. Maybe they wanted to learn about Jewish stuff, maybe they were scared, I don't know; but I was alone on the playground almost every Sunday. It was there that I perfected my NBA-worthy jump shot, my major-league slide into second, and my diving catch of the Super Bowl's winning throw.

By the time we got home, it was noon, and there was only one hour before the football games. We ate lunch and then tried to throw the ball around a little in our backyard to get into the mood. Then we settled in for some 1 p.m. Giants or Jets. My father wasn't a huge sports fan, but even he understood the importance of Sunday football. We weren't a close family;

we didn't usually have all the immediate relatives over for the games; but we did watch football together, and my mother would make food for us.

I wish I could tell you that these games were the beginning of a great bonding experience for my family. They weren't. It turned out to be the worst. While we could watch the 1 p.m. games in their entirety, the 4 p.m. games rolled around and the mood in the house changed with questions about homework and preparation for school: Did you take a bath or shower yet? Did you read a book today? Ugh!

Everyone knows that a football telecast takes about three hours, so the 4 p.m. games would end around 7, and then CBS aired *60 Minutes*. My parents watched *60 Minutes* like fat people feed their chocolate cravings. They never missed it. That meant that we kids had to have eaten dinner, done our chores, read a book, done our homework, and gotten ready for bed, all before 7 p.m. It also meant that we would not be watching the second half of the games.

So while all my buddies would be raving in school about this play or that play, or "Hey, did you see the way that game ended?" I wasn't. I could describe the first half, but when a game ended on a dramatic did-he-or-didn't-he kind of play and your best pals asked, "What did you think?" I was fucked.

There were days I got smart-assed and tried to explain to my folks that even God took Sunday off. That never worked. Are you God? Of course not; I'm just the lucky offspring who can't watch the fourth quarter of a damn Jets game because I have to be fed, washed, and in bed so you can watch *60 Minutes*. This routine went on even after I was bar mitzvahed and well into my teens.

My bar mitzvah, by the way, was one of the single worst days of my teenage years. I had to prep once a week for six months. Prep meant going to more Hebrew school to learn how to read certain passages of the Torah in Hebrew. It also meant learning several Hebrew songs that I would have to sing solo in front of everyone. The real problem, though, was the guest list. My parents were frugal, and they monitored the guest list the way Border Patrol agents guard against drug mules. I submitted the list of friends I wanted to invite, a solid mix of girls and guys. My father peered over it and came back to me with the following statement: "There are people on this list who have never been over to our house once; therefore they won't be invited. We have a limit, and if you invite all of these kids, we'll be over the number." The bad thing for me was that none of the girls on the list had ever been over to my house. Why would they have? I told my parents that the result would be no girls in attendance, but they didn't care.

A few months later, there I was at my bar mitzvah playing the game of Coke and 7-Up, which requires half the kids to be on one side of the dance floor facing the rest of the kids on the other side. Each kid has a partner, and when the DJ says "Coke," if you're on the Coke side, you run across the floor and sit on the lap of your 7-Up partner. It's a great game if there are girls on one side and boys on the other, but it's lousy when it's all boys. I had the worst bar mitzvah any thirteen-year-old with raging hormones could have ever had. Years later, just to see if he remembered, I asked my father why there weren't any girls there. He responded without blinking an eye: "Because you are ugly."

The older I got, the more conservative my parents got with the homework. While Monday came for everyone else at midnight, ours started at halftime in the late afternoon. I grew to hate Sundays, which was silly because then it only left me Friday nights and Saturdays. I dreaded the Sabbath because I knew I would either be in Hebrew school or getting ready for bed with the afternoon sun still out and my team still on the field.

The only thing I could do in protest was to root against my father's favorite teams. Although not a huge sports fan, he was your typical New Yorker. He was old-school, and that meant Giants football. It also meant the Dodgers until they moved out of Brooklyn; Knicks hoops; and to a far lesser extent, Rangers hockey. So in my second year of Hebrew school, I started rooting for the Jets. It was 1977, and they stunk.

Eight years removed from their only Super Bowl win—a game I have come to believe was fixed, to guarantee long-term prosperity for the NFL—I was now all in as a Jets fan. I picked a team with three wins to its name, no QB, no coach, and no place to call home. Dysfunctional just like me, the Jets had me at hello, and it's been a relationship that has served me well if for no other reason than it set the stage for some great character building.

There was no reason for an eight-year-old boy in New York to pick the Jets as his team, especially growing up in a Giants home. Except that the Giants stunk, too, so it wasn't like I had the choice of picking the front-running top team in town. I had to pick between two losers during the 1977 season—my dad's losers, or my own. There wasn't much I owned or could stake claim to back then. So the Jets were it.

WHY GUYS LOVE FOOTBALL

1. It's a violent sport with lots of scoring and bone-crushing hits, reminding us that it's in our DNA to rout and pillage.
2. We can gamble on it.
3. No matter how much of a ball and chain your wife or girl-friend is, she has to respect the fact that Sundays from Labor Day to February are yours to drink, gamble, hang with the guys, and act like a man on. She gets two Sundays anyhow—the first one's after the Super Bowl, and the second is Mother's Day—so she shouldn't bitch.

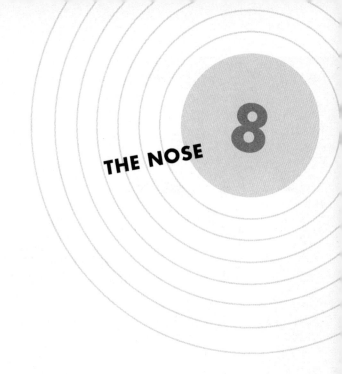

Life changed yet again in the spring of 1984, because clearly I had not experienced enough embarrassment, humiliation, and negativity in my life up to this point. I was fifteen years old and about to graduate from Albert Leonard Junior High School. I was still a few months way from having organized sports stolen from me by my grade-conscious parents, when they dropped another doozy on me.

Having been at the top of the junior high varsity soccer team in goals and assists, I was looking forward to the awards banquet at the end of the year. I knew that Jason Hadges and I would receive awards, and I was pumped for the event.

At that banquet we would receive our championship trophies for winning the league title; personal awards for goals, assists, and sportsmanship; and our official varsity letter, which most of our moms

would sew onto our varsity jackets. We got the jackets when we made the team, and the letters were special: a blue and white *A,* and an *L* with an orange soccer ball stitched inside the letters. You were allowed to invite whomever you wanted to the banquet because it was also a fund-raiser. My parents invited all of our relatives within twenty-five miles and, in typical generous Carton fashion, made each one of them pay their own entry fee to attend.

The downside of the banquet was that we didn't get to sit with our teammates. We had to sit with our families. So rather than messing around and hanging out, I had to endure an hour or so of family time, meaning I couldn't get up from the table for the duration of the event unless I was called up to the stage. My parents, brother and sister, aunt and uncle, and great-aunt and great-uncle were all at my table. I had gotten through the dinner portion of the night pretty well and thought I had clear sailing to the awards ceremony.

I will never forget what happened five minutes before I was called up to receive an award. My great-aunt Diana was sitting next to me chitchatting. I wasn't close with her, but my great-uncle was a cool dude who used to sell video games to big-box department stores, and he used to bring me along and pay me to demonstrate the games inside the store. It was a great job. For two hours I would sit in a reclining chair and play video games so other kids could see them and then ask their parents to buy them. It was brilliant marketing, and I would make twenty dollars each time I did it. He and I didn't have much in common, but I will never forget that he was cool enough to pay me to play video games.

So I was sitting at the table half-listening to my aunt Diana, and I went to take a sip of soda from the glass I was holding. I slowly brought the glass up to my face, my nose entered the inside of the glass, and I began to sip the drink. My aunt said, "Wow, you have a big nose. I'm surprised you could even take a sip out of that cup." I spit-gagged the soda, dumbfounded that she had said that—not to mention said it loud enough for everyone around us to hear.

My mother asked her to repeat what she had just said. Again without hesitation, Aunt Diana proclaimed, "Wow, he really has a big nose, and a funny mark on it, too."

My brother and sister thought this was hysterical, and then each person at the table started looking at me to judge for himself if I had a big nose, and what the mark on it was.

Then I heard ". . . and the award goes to Craig Carton!"

I walked up to the stage to accept the award. When I turned around to face the crowd, all I could think was that they all were staring at the big-nosed kid. I was right about one table for sure. Another great moment ruined, and the night hadn't even reached its peak of depressing.

When I was seven years old, my brother and I were horsing around with some toys, and we started to fight over who got to play with which one. My brother grabbed a toy truck that I wanted, and when I wouldn't relent trying to get it, he slammed it into my face—my nose, to be exact—and said "Here, take the truck!"

The truck slammed across the bridge of my nose and cut me, leaving a small discoloration from the scar. My parents took me to the doctor. I had a hairline fracture, but not to worry: the scar would go away over time, and the nose would repair itself as well. At the time I knew we should have had it checked out more thoroughly. They argued back and forth about what to do.

I had not given it another thought from that day on, and I had never once been told I had a big nose. My parents thought differently, though. The entire car ride home from the banquet had nothing to do with my award or getting my varsity letter; it had everything to do with my appearance. My mother was so distracted by my nose that to this day, she still has never sewed the letter on the jacket.

When we got home, I heard them contemplating what to do. They made calls to relatives to ask what they thought about the Nose and then decided what had to be done. I needed to have my nose fixed to accommodate for the fracture. It had not healed properly, they believed.

At no point did they ask me what I wanted to do. Later that night my mother came in to say good night to me and added, "We're going to see a doctor first thing tomorrow morning." I asked why, and she said, "To examine your nose." I told her that there was nothing wrong with it. It didn't hurt or bother me, and I was fine with it. "Good night," she said, and walked out of the room.

The next morning, to my dismay, my mother woke me up and told me to get in her car. We were off to New York City to see a nose specialist. He examined every angle of my schnoz and said I had some scar tissue from the original injury. If I wanted, he could fix it. I would even breathe better, he promised. My mother jumped on this one. This woman had forced me to get my tonsils out after two sore throats in first grade.

The doctor sensed that I wasn't into it, as I didn't say a single word during the entire exam. He asked if I was excited about what he was going to do. I said no. That brought on a whole new conversation between him and my mother about why this procedure was being done, but as a minor I had no say in the decision, and the doctor wasn't going to fight it. He was going to get paid, after all.

Forty-eight hours later, I was in an operating room about to have scar tissue removed from inside my nose, and the rest of my nose "fixed." I said nothing. I had learned to deal with everything on the inside, and that's what I did yet again. I let my parents dictate major aspects of my life without saying a word. I was counting down the days until I was eighteen and on my own.

When I entered the operating room, I wasn't nervous. I didn't say anything until right before they knocked me out. I remembered that before the doctors operated on President Reagan when he was shot by John Hinckley, he commented, "I hope you are all Republicans." I had no idea what a Republican was, but that story stuck with me. The guy could have died, but at least he had the presence of mind to be funny. I figured I'd try the same thing. Right before they put the gas mask on my face, I said, "I hope you are all Mets fans." Not a sound—nothing. Damn!

When I woke up, my nose was bandaged. The future looked bleak. The only thing that would have cheered me up was if I could have foreseen two weeks into the future, and known that soon I'd get to spend two hours dry-humping a curvaceous lifeguard.

PUT A GLOVE ON IT 9

Speaking of humping, let's be straight with one another: one of the perks of being a professional athlete is the opportunity to meet and sleep with tons of women. Hot chicks, ugly ones, skinny, fat—you name it. There is a sorority of women who will always be more than happy to oblige a famous athlete in the bedroom. What's amazing, though, is how many athletes are more than willing to oblige these gals in their pursuit of alimony, child support, and living the good life, years and years after what may have been a one-night romp.

I'll never forget the moment last year on *Hard Knocks* when New York Jets cornerback Antonio Cromartie struggled to name all of his kids. At the time, he only had ten children with eight different women. Then came the news this past spring that Antonio's on-again

wife was pregnant again, this time with twins. Antonio now has twelve kids: four with his current wife, and eight others with seven different women.

Unprotected sex feels better—no argument from me—but giving some random woman a couple of hundred grand a year for eighteen years because she saw herself as a celebrity semen collector makes rubbers sound hot. We should update *Fifty Shades of Grey* and put some condoms in the room. (Totally turned on now.) Antonio signed a four-year, $32 million contract with the Jets, so you would think that he could make the ridiculous monthly payments he is obligated to make. But more than that, unless his goal is to field an entire team made up of his DNA, he should either pull out or use condoms.

Cromartie ain't the only knucklehead handing out DNA lottery tickets. Charles Rogers, former number-two overall pick of the NFL draft in 2003 (and amazingly, out of the league two years later), received a total of $14 million in guaranteed bonuses. Figuring he would never run out of cash, he fathered five kids with four different women. I can only imagine how great that one gal who had two of his kids felt when all the moms got together. Sadly, though, Rogers was busted for hitting the weed pipe. Since that was a violation of his NFL contract, a judge ordered him to repay more than $6 million. Oops!

The all-time leader in this category is former Houston Rocket Calvin Murphy. He sired fourteen kids with nine different women. Murphy played professional ball in the 1970s, the era of the huge Afro and even huger pubic hair Afros, and was a onetime all-star. He was such a loving parent that as many as five of his daughters accused him in a court of law of abusing them. He was acquitted of those charges, but I suspect he doesn't receive any Father's Day gifts.

I heard of an Eagles player who came home after a strenuous workout without showering at the team facility. He was soaking wet and smelled like the garbage you'd find in the Hudson River. As he pulled into his townhouse parking lot, there was an attractive woman whom he had slept with several times before. She was waiting for him to come home so they could have sex. He gave her a quick hug and kiss and walked her into his home. She immediately went after him. He told her that he just came from working out and would gladly shower first, but she replied that she liked it dirty. He grabbed a condom and they had sex. Afterward he got up to discard the now-filled condom.

The groupie protested. "No reason to throw that out. That's for me for later," she said. God only knows what she had in mind. As nasty as it is, I hope she was going to drink it—although I wonder if she was going to inject it inside herself to try to get pregnant. You see, even when these guys try to do the responsible thing, sometimes it just doesn't matter.

Picture

this: A lanky teenage boy is standing just past the forty-yard line on a field that doubles for both football and soccer. He is sweating, having been in the summer sun for well over an hour. No more than twenty-five yards away, his high school varsity soccer team is playing on the same field. They are working on dribbling drills and corner kick plays. He knows every kid on the team. They are not only his best friends since first grade. Until a few weeks ago, they were his teammates.

The lanky kid figured he would be practicing alongside those kids. He was wrong, and now he's having his nose rubbed in it. An errant corner kick flies in his direction and stops maybe five feet away. His instinct is to kick it, but as the goalie runs toward the ball to retrieve it, the kid can only look away. Unsure if the goalie has figured out who

he is or what he is doing, he keeps his head down and kicks the ball hard and straight thirty yards away and into the goal. Now the goalie knows, and now he understands. "Hey, Craig, sorry man. Good luck."

"Carton!" screams the band leader. "We can't play 'I Feel Good' without you hitting the bass drum! Let's start again."

Why me?

By the time I got to ninth grade, which in our school system was still junior high, I had established myself as one of the premier soccer players not just in New Rochelle, but statewide as well. I was invited to join highly competitive travel teams. I was first or second in goals and in assists. As I entered tenth grade, I was psyched about playing varsity soccer alongside the kids I had been playing with since I was seven years old. I scored the winning goal in that famous multi-overtime game that was disallowed, and here we were about to enter high school and be varsity athletes. I knew we'd have a shot at advancing to the state championship every year we were there.

What I didn't know then was that I would never play a single game for New Rochelle High School, nor would I be a part of the senior team that did go on to win the state championship.

I graduated junior high with a B+ average, and took two Advanced Placement exams and got high 80s on both. Yet when the report card came home before the summer started, my parents reprimanded me for not taking school seriously. They warned me that there would be some changes when I got to high school.

As Labor Day neared, I got the phone call from the coach that late summer practice would be starting in advance of the school year. I told my parents, who replied that not only would I not go to the practices, but I wouldn't play soccer that year. It was time to "buckle down" and concentrate on my studies.

I was never anything less than a B+ student. While my parents were right that I didn't take school seriously, how many kids did? Unfortunately, my older brother did. He was a straight-A student class president and soon on his way to Dartmouth College. He is a great guy, and as well-rounded as a kid could have been: disgustingly strong academically, a solid athlete, and he never got into any trouble, unfortunately. That might explain why I once held a Swiss army knife to his throat when he wouldn't let me play ball with him and his friends, or why he never told my parents I did that.

If only he could be like his brother, my parents must have thought. I applied myself enough to get B-plusses, and I was content with that. I wasn't interested in studying, and I'm fortunate enough to have a limited photographic memory, so I just absorbed a lot of what I had to learn. If I'd buckled down, I could have been an A student, but why bother? My parents were the nothing-is-ever-good-enough types, particularly about grades, but I thought I didn't deserve to be punished. What normal tenth grader is looking ahead to the SATs or college choices—or anything other than girls and sports?

My parents were so crazy about schooling that my mother held the office of PTA president longer than any other human being in our district back then. She even handpicked all of my teachers before I got to opening day of first grade.

So here I was, a week away from entering high school, and I was forbidden from playing on the soccer team. To make matters worse, my parents decided that I had to take up a different extracurricular activity, so they forced me to be in the school band. I had to suffer the indignity of not just being in the marching band *and* the symphony band; I also had to practice marching moves on the same field that the soccer team sometimes practiced on. There I stood with this huge fucking bass drum attached to my body, as my closest pals played soccer twenty yards away.

What did I do in a previous life to deserve this? Why was I the only kid I knew who'd come home after getting a 92 on a difficult biology exam, only to have my folks say to him, "What happened to the other eight points?" My brother paved the way academically, so my parents thought that I should follow in his footsteps. The difference was, I didn't like raising my hand in class and didn't pay much attention to the teacher. Most of my time in school was spent daydreaming about playing center field for the Mets or playing soccer with Pelé.

When I was in fourth grade, my laziness caught up with me. I had a pop quiz on material that I did not remember reading, probably because I didn't. The teacher wanted to make sure that we were doing our assignments. I was as clueless as Snooki taking her SATs.

I did the best I could. The next day, when we got it back, I saw that I had got fourteen out of twenty questions right. I knew this wasn't going to fly. We had to get the tests signed by our parents. I thought of everything I could to get around the beating I would take if I came home with this test. I came up with something that turned out even worse.

I took Wite-Out and covered over four of the *x*'s.

The marks were written in green, for some reason. I whited them out with the precision of Leonardo da Vinci. I inspected them for hours before handing them to my parents. They knew I'd taken the test because they knew about every exam I ever took. After looking it over several times, they quizzically asked why the teacher wrote 14/20 when it appeared to them that I only got two wrong.

I donned my acting cap and said, "You're right! I got gypped." My parents said they would be escorting me to school the next day to find out what the problem was. I told them I would handle it. After all, it was just a quiz that didn't count against my overall grade. They were pissed, though, and wanted to know how this error could have happened.

I went to bed anxious, but resolute that I would walk in there with them in the morning anyhow and see what transpired. That would have been a terrible mistake, of course, but it never happened.

The next morning, as we were all eating breakfast, my father came down with a scowl on his face. He gripped the test so tightly that his fingers made dents in it. As I tried to gulp my orange juice, my father held the paper in the air and said, "I still can't believe this." As he did, the sunlight came through our kitchen window behind the paper. My mother said, "What is that?"

"What is what?" my father demanded. She said, "Look at the paper; it has something weird on it." The jig was up. My father turned the paper over and saw the Wite-Out from the backside.

There was no place to hide. There was no quick-witted story I could concoct. My father furrowed his brow and gave me the look that meant I was going to get the belt. Then he said something that has stayed with me: he wasn't as mad at me for what I had done with the Wite-Out as he was pissed that I was going to let them go to school and embarrass themselves by questioning the teacher's integrity.

"Why would you do that to me? What were you thinking?" The best I could offer was that I didn't want to get punished for getting a bad grade on a meaningless pop quiz. The saddest part was that no one else's parents even knew there was a quiz, but because my mom was czar of the PTA, she knew about each homework assignment and pop quiz. She knew when a teacher farted. I hated school because of it.

In sixth grade, it got even worse. My parents felt that I should follow in my brother's academic footsteps and be in the Advanced

Placement program. Sixth fucking grade—who cared about AP? I just wanted to play dodgeball. The teacher was a nice older woman named Mrs. Sciopelli, and she'd taught my brother. This was also a curse because not only did my parents expect me to live up to my brother's performance; now the teacher figured I should do so, too.

The first test we took, I was sitting next to Josh Kurzban. I had already decided that I would just copy his paper, since I knew nothing about what the test was on. So committed was I that I wrote "Josh Kurzban" where it asked for my name. That was a little hard to explain to Mrs. S.

At the end of the semester, we had a huge project that required three things: a written report, a verbal presentation, and a physical structure. Throughout the semester we had to give updates on our research to show we were doing the work. This project was supposed to take three months to complete. I did nothing. My topic was the relationship between lords and serfs in medieval times. When we had to do our last update in class one-on-one with the teacher, I had nothing. She gave me an F.

I went home thinking I had at least escaped my folks' finding out, that is, until the phone rang in the middle of Friday dinner. I was only three forks into my spaghetti and meatballs when my mother answered the call, listened for a minute, then looked at me and said, "Oh really, is that so?" I knew who was on the phone and what was being said. I even knew what the punishment would be. I knew my weekend was ruined.

I was sequestered in my room from Friday night through Sunday night, only allowed out for meals and bathroom breaks. In two and a half days, I did the entire project that took everyone else three months. I even built a huge castle with a moat, fake trees, water, and people. I brought it in on Monday, the day it was expected, and killed with the presentation. I deserved an A but only got a B because I rushed it in three days.

This lesson may have been valuable, but it was not the one my parents wanted me to learn. I learned that I could do well in school without doing the legwork. That worked out fine for me until they decided I couldn't play soccer in high school. Later, when I was applying to colleges, I still had a good enough reputation to be invited to some schools for visits by the coaches. But by then I had lost my interest in soccer altogether, and was running an illegal living room casino and dating a *Playboy* centerfold.

HELLO, PRINCETON! 11

Barely a day goes by that the athletic world isn't affected by one type of scandal or another. At the collegiate level, typically it's in relation to star athletes either cheating on exams, having someone take those exams for them, or passing classes without even taking exams. When I was a junior at Syracuse, I had access to the athletic facilities set aside for scholarship athletes. Not because I was one, but because I had played club baseball my freshman year there. As a result, I had a pass that never expired.

One day when I was walking through the locker room after playing ball, I saw a note stuck to every mirror. The note said, "Psych 205 students: If you need a copy of the midterm, see Joe." There was a telephone number there as well. I had Psych 205, so I called the number,

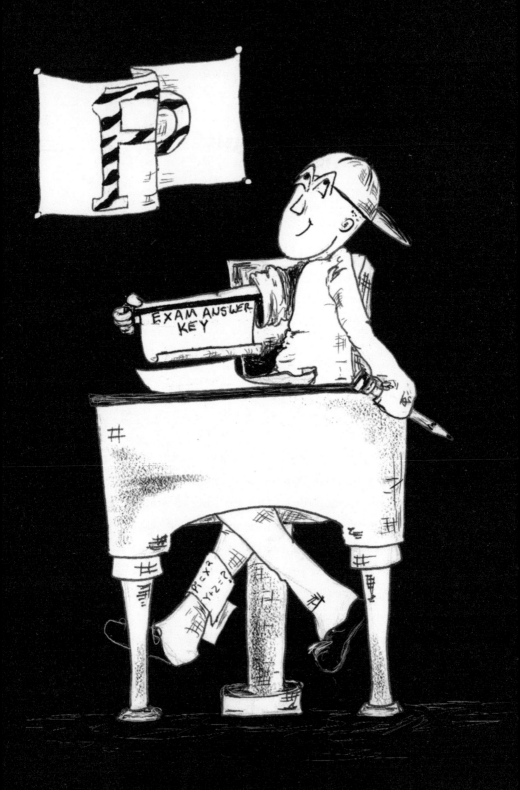

and within thirty minutes some random guy came and gave me the midterm that I would be taking in a few days.

My studying, as little as it was, came to a halt. I began solely to study the questions on the test. This was before the Internet, so professors reproduced their tests on old copier machines and the carbon copy that was left behind contained the test. Someone had gotten hold of it and made copies for the athletes so that they could pass it. In theory, you didn't even have to study the questions and learn the answers. You only needed someone else to know the answers and give them to you, and then you just had to memorize the order: A, D, C, A, etc.

A few days later, I sat for the test. It was the exact test I had in my possession days earlier. I purposely got some questions wrong so it wouldn't look like I had cheated. It was a tough class, after all.

The following week, we were supposed to get our grades back. The professor walked in. He was pissed. He announced that he had learned that someone had stolen a copy of the test before he administered it. The entire test we took was now void. He would be giving us a new test right now, and it was the hardest test he had ever created. He guaranteed us that no one would get over a 40. I was crushed, and only hoped he'd be grading on a curve. Thankfully he did, and my 58 was actually a B+ because everyone else did so badly.

While you might expect this kind of thing at a hugely successful Division 1A sports school, you wouldn't expect it at an Ivy League school.

Wrong.

As the basketball team at Harvard has gotten better and better under coach Tommy Amaker, they have apparently also gotten envious of ball players at non–Ivy League schools who don't have to study. Even worse for the Ivy Leaguers is that they are not offered sports scholarships. They have to pay, *and* they have to study. Damn the injustice.

In late summer of 2012, nearly half of the 279 students in a government course were embroiled in a cheating scandal. Included in the mix was Kyle Casey, the leading scorer on the men's basketball team. He has since withdrawn from school, and fellow co-captain Brandyn Curry did, too. Why withdraw from school, though? Well, withdrawing before the school year allowed them to retain an extra year of eligibility to play.

Hello, Princeton!

What's next? Crib notes at the Scripps Spelling Bee?

SCHOOL TRIPPING 12

In September 1986, I was a senior in high school. I still had not focused on what colleges I wanted to apply to. I wasn't all that worried about it, though. I assumed I would figure it out eventually. But I didn't have to worry. My parents had already begun the process of choosing a school for me. I had given up trying to emancipate myself from my parents. I just went with the flow.

This attitude had started years ago, and it was now serving me well. I mean, what seventeen-year-old allows his parents to control every aspect of his life without the slightest bit of rebellion? Maybe I was lazy, or maybe I was a big pussy afraid to challenge the authority of my parents. Regardless, while my buddies applied frantically to dozens of colleges and universities across America, I didn't.

I applied to only five schools, and of them, I only picked one

myself. My parents wanted me to follow in my brother's footsteps and go to an Ivy League college, but my grades weren't of that caliber, and I didn't want them to be. As a high school senior I visited my brother at Dartmouth. I saw that his course load was ridiculous, plus they were on a trimester setup, so he had to go to school for what seemed like the entire year. I also didn't care for the other kids I met up there—all booshie and pretentious—and the girls weren't pretty. The Ivies were out.

My most memorable experience at an Ivy League school was being in Hanover, New Hampshire, for my brother's graduation from Dartmouth. The night before he graduated, his fraternity had a big party, as did all the other frat houses. Most of the kids had lined up a guaranteed 100K job, or graduate school. Looking back on it now, the idiots I graduated with—myself included—had no job prospects, much less making big bucks. A life of gay porn was a more likely pursuit.

My parents, my sister, and I drove up to New Hampshire with my aunt, uncle, and grandma trailing along. My sister and a girlfriend of hers went to the party with me. At this stage of my life, I could already hold my drink, having learned the skill at Gary's Barleycorn in New Rochelle, just a few blocks from the Iona College campus. We hit the frat party and said yes to every shot and stale beer served to us in the basement of the house. I will never forget the smell of cheap brew, or the sound of Ping-Pong balls hitting sixteen-ounce plastic cups during a marathon game of beer pong. I'll also never forget hearing "Hang On, Sloopy" forty-seven times in a row.

Drinking wasn't the only thing I was good at. I had developed a complete disregard for my own welfare when it came to fighting. Don't get me wrong, I didn't get in a lot of fights, but I didn't mind stepping up to someone looking for one, nor did I back down from a guy who deserved to get his ass kicked.

After playing beer pong with random dudes and chicks for a while, I went upstairs and found my brother playing a game of pool. I grabbed another beer—probably my eighth—and watched. As my brother started draining balls all over the table, I noticed that the demeanor of his opponent was getting worse.

The kid was drunk. His face got tighter and redder with each perfect strike of the cue ball from my brother. My spidey senses started to tingle all over. The kid was about to snap. With four balls to go, my brother hit a sweet bank shot and I saw the dude grab his pool cue with two hands like it was a bat. I moved right next to him so he could feel my hip bumping up against his. It distracted him from my brother, which was my goal. I wasn't done.

I was drunk, and happy to engage with this douchebag. I leaned into his ear and said something witty, like "If you take one step toward him with that stick, I'll drive it so far up your ass, you'll be spitting wood for a month."

The kid looked at me and said, "Fuck you, who the fuck are you?"

Game on.

He pushed his hand into my chest. I pulled him to the ground, got on top of him, and put my hands around his throat. In my best Rambo voice, I said, "I could really fuck you up. Now when I get up, don't be an asshole." By that time my brother and a few of his frat brothers came rushing over, pulled me off him, and told me to go home.

I went downstairs, got into the family station wagon with my sister and her friend, and began the twenty-minute drive back to the Holiday Inn. I was buzzed, no doubt about that, but I mistakenly thought that I had reinvigorated my senses during the nonfight and thought I was fine to drive. The brisk nighttime New Hampshire air also seemed to help.

I was wrong, of course. On the way home, I drove over the curb twice before straightening out the car. As I made it to the street that the hotel was on, I saw the big green sign about a quarter mile ahead. I put on my turn signal and started to make a left. The problem was that the sign was about 250 yards before the actual entrance to the parking lot. I was now crossing a double yellow onto the off-ramp of a major highway.

I realized what I was doing and turned hard, back across the double yellow and onto the right side of the road. Within a few seconds, I saw police lights behind me.

I pulled into an empty gas station, the cop following me. I had never been pulled over before, drunk or sober. As a virgin at this, I didn't know what I was supposed to do. So I did the worst thing possible. I put the car in park, opened my door, and started to jog toward the cruiser. My sister and her friend thought the whole thing was hysterical and couldn't stop laughing. I could have strangled them both.

The police officer was halfway out of his car as I began my jog. He grabbed his gun, got into a two-point stance, and hollered, "Freeze!" He had every reason to shoot me. I raised my hands and said, "Yes, sir. Sorry, sir." He barked at me to get back in my car and to put my hands on the steering wheel. I was frozen with the gun pointed at me, but he wasn't putting it away until I obeyed. I went back to my car. My sister and her friend were still laughing like hyenas, and I kept trying to make them shut up.

The officer came to the car, asked for license and registration, and went back to his vehicle. More hilarity from the girls, more time passing, and more worrying by me. After ten minutes that felt like an hour, he came back to the car and asked me what we were doing. I explained that my brother was graduating the next day, and we were coming back from a family dinner. He of course asked if I had been drinking, and I said I'd had two beers with my meal.

He explained in detail how he had been following me for miles and saw me hit the two curbs, and then he told me to get out of the car. He didn't give me a Breathalyzer, thank God, but he did give me a road-side sobriety test. Hand out, index fingers to the nose, recite the alphabet, and then the hardest part: close your eyes, tilt your head back, and touch your nose without wobbling, followed by heel-to-toe walking a line. After the test, he told me to get back in the car and asked me where I was staying. I told him the Holiday Inn right next door. He asked if my parents were there. I said that not only were they there, but they were sleeping, and I'd rather he not wake them up.

"Follow me to the hotel," he responded. He drove first, lights on, and I followed as instructed. When we got in front of the lobby, he came to my window and asked me my father's first name and told me he was waking him up to tell him what happened so my dad would make sure I stayed in my room the rest of the night.

It was three in the morning. There ain't nothing to do in New Hampshire at that time of night unless you're cow-tipping, or making the walk of shame back home from a fat girl's house. He went inside the hotel, spent about five minutes in there, and came out alone. He said, "I'm not going to tell your dad, but do all of us a favor and don't drive when you drink. Now go to bed, and enjoy your brother's graduation."

I thanked him, and my sister and I swore each other to secrecy on the evening's events. We crept back to our rooms and went to bed. We kept that secret until the following Thanksgiving, when my sister told the whole story to everybody in my family.

Now, less than a year later, I sat in a car with my mom and dad on our way to Boston to check out Tufts. I wanted nothing to do with Tufts, but they insisted on my applying to Ivy League schools, and Tufts was as close as I could get. I was miserable and uncomfortable, like the first time your parents take you shopping for a suit and make you try on nine of them on a sunny Saturday afternoon while you'd rather be outside. After a whole day spent touring Tufts and getting the academic load, my parents looked at each other and said, "This is where you should be."

I told them I had no interest in it. But they had this amazing superpower whereby they could turn their hearing off and become deaf when I spoke. On the long ride back, they contemplated aloud what I should write my essay about, and whether I would be—excuse me, *they* would be—applying early.

Applying early meant that you sent in the application to the school of your choice in the fall, and by late January you could find out if you were accepted or not. Within forty-eight hours of our returning from Tufts, my application was in the mail. I was now just a few months away from potentially being in a college that I wanted no part of. If you do not get in, you have to hedge your bets, so they sat me down to ask what other schools I was interested in.

I hadn't given it any thought. They chimed right in with "How about Colgate, Ithaca, Hamilton, and Hobart?" Hamilton was an easy choice because its soccer coach had been involved in Westchester soccer and knew about me before my folks banned me from playing. While they didn't offer scholarships per se, they did offer me a merit-based scholarship to play soccer.

The good news about these schools was that they were all close to one another, so theoretically, visiting them could be done in one easy trip. My dad decided that he and I would go on a father-son road trip to see each of those schools in early October.

Of course, he chose a day that the Mets were in a playoff game. He didn't care one bit about the Mets or sports in general. There was no arguing with him. Bright and early on a Saturday morning, we got into the car at six o'clock and started out toward Ithaca, New York, on the road trip of all road trips. The idea was that we would see three or four of the schools that day, find a shitty motel to stay in, hit one more the next morning, and return home. The problem with the plan was that my father and I had nothing to talk about.

We got in the car and began our trek to a never-before-seen part of upstate New York. I adjusted the radio, and my father yelled at me for it being too loud and turned it off. I turned it back on, lowered it, and settled in to Bon Jovi singing "Livin' on a Prayer."

"What is this noise? Turn it off!"

This was going to be a long trip.

I leaned against the window, hoping to fall asleep. Before my head made contact with the pillow I'd brought along, I heard, "You're not going to fall asleep and leave me all alone."

It was a four-hour drive to Ithaca, and other than a few awkward attempts at small talk, we made it all the way without a single meaningful conversation. This could have been the most amazing father-son road trip. He could have gotten creative and agreed to hit some bars or strip clubs along the way. He could have opened up and told me some great college stories from his days at Alfred. Instead, he wanted to discuss what kind of time we were making.

Maybe it's a Jewish thing, but it seems that my people are overly concerned with making good time on car voyages. Everywhere we went, there was always some sort of inevitable conversation among the adults about it: "What kind of time did you make?" "Oh, we made great time." Well, we were making good time that morning, and it seemed to make my dad happy.

I don't want to be too hard on him. It's not like I was engaging him in dialogue, either. Here we were, two closed-off peas in a pod, driving endlessly. The one thing my father didn't know yet was that there would be no motel, there would be no staying over. Most important, there would be no missing the Mets playoffs. There would be, however, more miles driven in a single day by any Carton in the history of the family.

We visited the Ithaca campus, and then on to Hamilton and Hobart. At Hamilton we met with the soccer coach, got a tour of the athletic facilities, and enjoyed lunch in the student dining hall.

The biggest issue was that both schools required a fifty-page essay on one of four different topics. I would have to write this essay in addition to my regular homework and turn it in with my application. They lost me right there. If I had to do a fifty-page anything just to be considered for admission, imagine how much work I'd have to do once I got there. I wasn't looking for a school that required me to do a lot of work. I was looking for high school extended; a place where I could do enough to get a solid B average and spend the rest of the time having fun.

We had no plans to visit Syracuse, and after seeing Ithaca, Hamilton, and Hobart, and enduring the silent driving treatment, I was good to go home. My father looked at his map and said, "If we make good time, we can hit Colgate, too." So off we were to Colgate. Another brief walk through campus, and then an executive decision by my dad that changed the course of my life for the better. He decided that since we were there and we'd never do this again, we should check out Syracuse, too. "Okay," I said, and off we went.

Of the five schools that I visited, Syracuse was the only one I didn't set foot in. We drove through campus, and I saw the frat houses and the quad and tons of hot chicks. We never stopped to get out.

I had found my home. Great sports, big school, and enough

great-looking babes that even I should be able to disappoint at least one a week. It was four in the afternoon when we were done with our drive-by of the 'Cuse, and we had to make a decision: find a motel, grab dinner and crash, or be daring.

My dad is competitive like me, so I tweaked him by saying there was no way he could get us home that night in time to watch the Mets-Astros playoffs. If he did, I would buy dinner and Baskin-Robbins ice cream. If he didn't make it, he'd have to pay. To his credit, he got us there by the top of the third, drove more than seven hundred miles in one day, engaged me in zero conversation about anything (other than how we were making good time), and deserved the fudge brownie ice-cream sundae I had to buy him when we returned.

IF SHE LOOKS TOO YOUNG, SHE IS

13

There have been lots of stories of athletes getting in trouble by dating or sleeping with teenage girls. Now, most of us have had experience with teenagers, but it was when we were teens ourselves, or in our early twenties dating eighteen-year-olds. We aren't, however, pro athletes with tons of cash and the celebrity status that all girls, not just teens, find attractive. The problem is, for pro athletes (as it is for all of us), it's unacceptable to be wooing, dating, or banging a teenager *unless they have been dating since college.* Which would still put the girl on the young end of the scale when they first started going out.

I will never forget two of my own experiences with teenage girls.

The summer before my senior year of high school was eventful. I lost my virginity that summer. Sadly, though, it wasn't filled with romantic music or the seek-and-destroy type of love story that we know

from the movies. Nope. My first time took place in the front seat of my parents' Chevy Caprice classic wagon, and yes, there was fake wood attached on the outer side panels. The real wood was attached to me. I had messed around with plenty of girls but had never found the right one. Either I wasn't making the right moves, or I had picked the wrong girls.

The last girl I dated before I got the job done was a girl from Westchester County. She was a lifeguard at the camp where I was a counselor. She had the single greatest body any sixteen-year-old has ever had, and other than a slightly hooked nose, she was stunning. We had fooled around after camp in my car or hers for a few weeks, and there was a connection.

One late summer night, she decided to have a small house party with five girls and five of the guy counselors. Everyone knew I was with her, so the other fellas had to worry about partnering off with a girl of their own. After doing some shots of J.D. followed by Bud chasers we were all feeling pretty good. Then the wine coolers came out. That's right—wine coolers. None of us had ID good enough to walk into a liquor store and get booze, so we had to settle for whatever was left of her dad's Jack. We then replaced it with cola, figuring that by the time he came home to drink it, it would be flat and look like whiskey. The beer came from one of the guys' older brothers, and there wasn't much of it. So Bartles & Jaymes it was, topped off by a little Seagram's from her dad's stash.

After making an outdoor fire in one of those pits you always want to order when you're flipping through the SkyMall catalog, it was time to make my move. I grabbed her hand and told her to come with me. We went inside and starting making out in the kitchen. Luckily I didn't shoot a geyser right then and there. I was so hard, I could have popped a hole through both our pants. First base, all good, and now on to second base. Hands creeping under the shirt, attacking the rack like it stole something.

Then it happened. She said, "Let's go to my bedroom." YESYES YESYES! I was going to get laid! Two condoms had been gathering dust in my wallet since my bar mitzvah, nearly three years earlier. I had considered putting new ones in there, just so it wouldn't look like they had been there forever.

Up to the bedroom we went, and onto her bed. I was now tired of her boobs and ready for the treasures that lay in wait elsewhere. I slowly moved my hand past her belly button, and began trying to pry my fingers past her belt. What the fuck! I tried and tried, but I barely got my hand halfway down her pants. This being the days before woman got Brazilians, I felt some Chewbacca action, and I knew I was getting close.

If I felt that today, I would tell my wife to get a wax immediately. How we used to tolerate a hairy bush I will never know, but I blame it on our parents. That whole free-love, 1960s bullshit spanned damn near three more decades of women thinking it was all right to have Dr. J in a leg lock. My boys are blessed. When they're grown, they will never have to know what it's like to part a woman's lower Afro to reach the Promised Land.

Anyhow, this girl had a tourniquet around her waist, so I did the next best thing. My middle finger made it down there and even inside a little bit, while I dry-humped her for an hour. I was hard the whole time, but it got to a point where it wasn't even sexy. We made out as I played nonstop with her boobs, and then finally I got bored and said we should go back downstairs. When I got home, I had blue balls the size of the Rock of Gibraltar. I limped around all weekend, even after taking care of business myself.

Fast-forward six weeks. There I was, getting it on in my car with a girl from a rival high school, whom I'd met at a house party. There was no way I would be denied this time. Rumor had it that she was easy. We had been drinking for a few hours when I knew I had to get her home. It turns out her dad was anti-Semitic, and if I dropped her off at her house, I would have to meet him. If I did, he would ask if I was Jewish, and that would put the kibosh on our plans. So she told me to park two blocks down, in front of some random house. Within two minutes, my pants were around my ankles, and we got the job done.

When you are sixteen, it's okay to do whatever it takes to try to land another sixteen-year-old. But when you are Lawrence Taylor, Mark Sanchez, or dozens of others, it is not.

Let's take LT first. In 2010, LT was arrested for "sexual assault of a minor" after he ordered a hooker to his hotel room following a golf course appearance. Now, we all know that LT is a scumbag from the drugs and his multiple arrests. He ain't a good guy. Ordering a hooker, in and of itself, isn't a problem to me. I think it ought to be legalized. But LT took it to another level. The girl who showed up that night was fifteen years old. I don't care who you are, when you are fifty and experienced with women, there's no way you aren't clear that the naked girl in front of you is a kid. I realize that girls today are developing more rapidly than ever, and some even could be confused for an of-age woman when they're all dolled up, but there is no way you can't tell that a fifteen-year-old is too young.

Lawrence should be thrown in jail for life and never seen again. There are those who make the argument that he had the right to assume the hooker was of age, since when did hookers come with licenses proving their age? It's a dumb argument; it makes me want to puke and then spit it on the people that make it.

The difference between Mark Sanchez and LT is so glaring that it also bothers me when people compare them. Sanchez was in a club where you had to be twenty-one even to enter the place. Now, I know the law does not excuse ignorance as a defense, but at first he did nothing wrong. He simply met a good-looking girl.

Mark is an incredibly handsome dude, and the chick he picked up, and I imagine (but don't know for a fact) hooked up with all night, was attractive for an average high school chick from Connecticut. But in terms of the starting QB of the Jets, who could bang any New York City model and probably has a few under his belt, this chick was a five on the Carton chick-rating scale.

Mark met the girl at the club and took a liking to her, and he asked her how old she was. She said, "I'm seventeen." His first response was perfect: He said, "Sorry, you're too young. Call me in a year." If he had only left at that point, all would be good, but she must have grabbed his cock or stuck a finger in his ass, because he didn't leave after telling her goodbye. She responded by saying "I'm legal. It's seventeen in New York and sixteen in Jersey." Again, she was telling the truth. You must hand it to her for doing her homework. She could have done her senior thesis on the topic. Factual and practical, the girl knew what she was doing.

Since apparently she was Phi Beta Kappa, Mark took her at her word and left the club with her. I mean, would a girl lie about that when she has the chance to bed down the starting QB of any team, let alone the Jets? They went back to his place, and did what I imagine came naturally. Then he must have gone to shower, and that's when he made his second mistake. He left a teenage girl alone in his apartment with complete access to his shit. She of course took pictures. I mean, I would have. He's Mark fucking Sanchez, for crying out loud!

At some point she went home, and then he made his third mistake.

He started texting her and calling her late at night after playoff games. Her response to one text when he asked her to come over at 3 a.m. was, "Sorry Mark, I have school tomorrow—high school." Too funny. Nothing like being horny and having your girlfriend cock-block you because she's studying for her SATs.

She must have been good in bed, because then he took her out on a date. Brutal decision, because now you can't even deny anything. As you know, he got photographed by TMZ or some other photographer when he walked into the restaurant. At some point he must have turned his brain on and figured out that banging a seventeen-year-old was bad for his image. He called it off, and she did what any normal person would do: she e-mailed Deadspin.

While what he did was stupid and amoral, it wasn't illegal. Life goes on, but we can all learn some valuable lessons from LT and Mark Sanchez:

1. If she looks too young, she is.
2. If a girl says to you, "I'm legal," run.
3. Don't ever take a teenager out to dinner.
4. You can't trust a hooker.

Not that I haven't spent some time with hookers myself.

Bob Murphy and the Mets made me forget my encounter with a hooker.

I don't deny spending lots of time with strippers and Hooters girls throughout my life, but I've never paid for sex. Let me clarify that statement: I never once paid a working woman solely for sex. We have all paid for sex in some way, and we have done it a lot. Every time you take a woman out for drinks or buy her dinner, you do it with a goal in mind, and that goal isn't to find a soul mate or a best friend. Instead, it's: "I hope this date ends with us in bed naked."

Sex was the one and only goal of every date I ever went on:

Showering before the date: SEX
Cologne on entire body: SEX

Opening the door for her to get in the car: SEX

Stopping at a bar before dinner: SEX

Nice restaurant for dinner: SEX

Nightcap after dinner: SEX

Tickets to a sporting event: SEX

Rollerblading: SEX

Hansom cab in Central Park: SEX

Walking her to her apartment door: SEX

Pretending to love her poodle: SEX

Pretending to be interested in what she has to say: SEXSEXSEX

All of it is geared toward getting laid. So I have paid for sex—you bet your ass I have—but I never paid a girl expecting cash for sleeping with me. There's a big difference. I have been in the company of hookers, and despite never having received "favors" from them, I could have if things had played out differently.

For me, sex was never emotional or deep. Sex was important to me, but more as a conquest and a challenge. Don't get me wrong; I enjoy it, and every now and then I am good at it, but I am often removed from the sensual personal act of sleeping with another person. Being with a hooker would appear to be the perfect sexual outlet for me, but I find the concept of paying for sex disgusting. As a kid who grew up with the specter of Magic Johnson and AIDS, I worried about contracting the disease. I had no problem being with strippers and Hooters girls. While I'd be lying if I said that every one I went out with was premed or wanted to be a lawyer and was paying her way through school, I did feel that they were in a different category from hookers.

The first time I ever saw a real hooker was when I was seventeen years old. I was a counselor at a summer camp with my best friend, Steven. We both became friends with a kid named Mike. One summer night we were drinking in Steven's basement, and we were debating what to do for the night. We called a few of the female counselors to come over to Steven's house and swim in his pool and party, but they couldn't come over until later in the night. So we planned for them to come over at ten. However, it was only seven, and the idea of the three of us drinking alone for several hours didn't seem too intriguing. Going to a bar with our lousy fake IDs just to prime ourselves for the night seemed like a bad idea. And then Mike announced, "I know what we can do! Let's go get blowjobs."

Now, he didn't say, "Let's go get blowjobs from a hooker." He just said, "Let's go get blowjobs." At seventeen, I wasn't going to say, "No, that's a lousy idea," and neither was Steven. I had recently been devirginized and was eager for more. The idea that I could just get into a car and drive somewhere and some chick would blow me seemed great. The three of us jumped into Mike's car, and he started to drive. I'm not sure if it was me or Steven, but at some point one of us asked where we were going.

Mike smiled, said, "I know just the spot," and cranked up the Zeppelin tape. About fifteen minutes into the ride, it was clear that we were going toward Manhattan, so I lowered the radio and asked again if we were going to a club or to some chick's house he knew. He looked over at me and said, "We're going to find a hooker." This concept, which just twenty minutes earlier seemed like the greatest notion ever, now seemed like the single dumbest idea of all time. A hooker? "For real?" I asked. Mike reassured me, "I do it all the time. It's totally cool. Don't worry. I know where to go."

I was worried and scared at the same time. Going back to Steven's house and waiting for the girls to show up seemed like a much better idea. I started to pepper Mike with questions, so much so that he got annoyed with me. We wound up driving close to Times Square and started cruising down the street in the mid-forties between Tenth Avenue and Broadway.

After about seven trips up and down, we found her, a lone figure in high heels and a ridiculously short miniskirt and black leather jacket. She was walking with her back facing away from traffic, looking at cars as they drove past. Driving slowly was a sign that we were looking to conduct business. She came over to the window. Mike said, "Three blowjobs," so matter-of-factly that I was surprised. I thought there might be some pleasantries beforehand, but it was right to business. I heard her say something like "Just you, or all of you?" and he said, "Three of us. How much?"

I didn't get to hear the rest of the conversation, but it went well enough for her to tell Mike to pull over halfway down the street, turn his lights off, then have two of us get out of the car, as she would take care of us one by one. Mike volunteered to go first, which was just fine with me. I was desperate to not go at all. This was one of the those early male-bonding situations where you don't want to do something, but if pressed, you are going to have to do it. If you don't, you can no longer be trusted.

Two things concerned me. The first was the police. It would be just my luck if the first time I ever got arrested, it was for getting a blowjob from a hooker. The thought of being arrested, going to jail, and making that phone call home unnerved me. I started to pace while Mike was in the car. Every now and then I looked over and saw the woman's head going up and down, which made me even more antsy.

The second thought that unnerved me was whether I would be able to get it up. At that age, I spent most of every day with some sort of hard-on, but for once my little guy wasn't in the mood. I started to try to imagine my favorite *Playboy* model naked. No dice. I tried to stimulate myself through my pocket. No dice . . . What was I going to do? There had to be nothing worse than being kicked out of the car by a hooker because she has nothing to work with. I played every imaginable sexy scenario in my mind. Each one made it worse.

And then, as if it were a gift from the gods, it happened. The car door flew open. At the same time I heard Mike yell, "What the fuck?" The hooker leaned her head out the door and start puking all over the side of the road, the car, and Mike. Vomit was everywhere.

I had my out.

There was no way I was going to let this hooker blow me now. Thankfully, there was no way she wanted to anyhow. She got out of the car still heaving, which made me start to heave as well. There is nothing worse than the smell of vomit. She limped to the curb. We got into the car. Thank God it was summer, and we could roll the windows down for the drive home, although even that didn't help.

Mike was livid. Not only didn't he get to finish the blowjob, but his car stunk. Nobody was in the mood for Zeppelin or for anything else. Most things that happen to guys we can laugh about and break each other's balls over, but that night all of us were silent. We all agreed to put the Mets game on the radio. This was the summer of 1986, so the Mets, who were closing in on winning the National League East, were playing the Expos at Shea.

On the way into the city we had checked the game on the radio a few times, but nothing grabbed our attention. On the way home, though, it became clear that we might be the three luckiest guys in the world ever to have a hooker vomit in their car. When we turned the radio on, Bob Ojeda hadn't let up a single hit. The Mets had never had a no-hitter in their franchise's history. Here we were, about to catch it on the radio.

Ojeda took the no-hitter into the seventh, and we were all jacked up and talking again. The hooker was no longer important. We were

Mets fans, and we were cheering our asses off. We were about ten minutes away from New Rochelle, and if Ojeda could get through the seventh, we could watch the rest of the game on TV. John sped his car along the Hutchinson River Parkway as Ojeda got the first Expo out. Next up was light-hitting Luis Rivera. As he came to the plate, we got off the parkway and were now just two miles away from home and history, when *Wham!* With one out in the seventh, Luis Rivera singled. Two batters later, he scored to tie the game. Shit!!

We had to be the only three guys to fuck up blowjobs and a no-hitter, all in the same night.

We did have three girls coming over, though, so we tried to prep ourselves by jumping in the pool and making sure we didn't smell like puke. John parked his car two blocks away, just in case the girls decided to check it out. We brought a radio outside so we could listen to the rest of the game while we drank and waited for the girls.

The Mets went back in front in the bottom of the eighth when Ray Knight doubled in two runs. Ojeda got the leadoff man in the ninth, but then gave up three straight singles. Roger McDowell came in and blew the save by giving up a hit to Andre Dawson. Ray Knight came through again, singling in the winning run with two outs in the tenth off Tim Burke. As the Mets players mobbed each other, the three of us cheered with shots of Jack in Steven's hot tub with the three counselors, who more than made up for our misadventure in the city just a few hours earlier.

Jack Nicklaus set me up with my second encounter with a hooker.

I know. You're thinking: there's no way the golf legend set me up with a prostitute. But in a weird way, he did.

For three straight summers, starting after senior year in high school, I had a job with a valet parking company. It was run by a small, neb-bishy Jewish kid who was the son of a wealthy parking garage magnate. Its main account was the booshie Westchester Country Club, as blue-blood a facility as there is in the world; all old money, and an average membership age of well over fifty.

Some of my buddies and I got wind that kids our age were making a shitload of money working there. We applied and were hired. Most days, our routine was routine: people pulled in for dinner, we parked

their cars and waited for the wealthy elderly people to finish eating, and then we retrieved their vehicles. For most of these people, the car of choice was an old Caddy the size of a small pontoon, or the classic Mercedes. In either case, the cars smelled like old people and old cigars, or a combination of both. There were many times I would take a deep breath just before entering the car and try to hold it until I was out. We would run about a half mile to the lot where we'd parked their cars and drive them back to the entrance, collect a modest tip, and do it all over again. This shift usually lasted from 5 p.m. until 2 a.m., but the real work was from 6 to 8 p.m. and then again from 10 p.m. to midnight, when the diners arrived and departed, respectively. In between, we got high, played cards, threw a ball around, and tried to pass the time without getting too bored.

Wednesday nights were bonus nights for us, as it was Lobster Night. We'd roll out of there with a minimum of $150 a man, which was what we made on weekends. But the event we all waited for was the annual PGA tour event the Buick Classic. Not only did we get to meet the golf pros, but we made at least $500 a day, and the tourney was four days long. All cash, of course, and you earned every penny because you ran nonstop all day.

Buick, the title sponsor of the event, provided the courtesy cars for all the golfers and major sponsors. During the tournament, we had to get to the course by 6 a.m. and stay till nearly midnight. It involved constant running and parking and driving cars, but again, it was well worth it. It was a coveted gig to be able to greet the drivers and then bring the cars down to the club, because there were some kids who spent all day in the open lot doing the actual arranging and parking. Those guys got a set rate for the day, but those of us who were lucky enough to meet the cars when they arrived could make big bucks.

I often look back on that week of my life, and that $2,000. When I got my first job in Buffalo, New York, at WGR Radio, I made $12,000 for the year, and that was before taxes. That's a grand a month. Two months' work on the radio paid the same amount that I made in cash in four days of parking cars. The first day of the tournament, I arrived at the club by 6 a.m. The day was going great, steady running and driving. Days like that go fast, as opposed to nights waiting for the three remaining octogenarians to finish gumming their lobster tails and come out to get their cars. By 4 p.m., my pockets bulged with cash. Then a young, Waspy-looking guy wearing a Buick-logoed golf shirt and khakis came out, cut the line, and handed me a parking ticket. "This is Mr. Nicklaus's car; get it fast. He doesn't like to wait," he said.

I was off. I was fetching the car of the Golden Bear, the greatest golfer to ever live (before Tiger, of course, and with all due respect to Arnold Palmer, who many people feel was better than both of them). I wondered if I was going to meet him, or just give the keys to one of his lackeys, like the guy who gave me the ticket.

I had met two other notable athletes in my time at Westchester Country Club prior to this moment. I was never a star-fucker, never a big autograph guy, but even for me, meeting Ralph Branca and Bobby Thomson a few months earlier on Lobster Night was cool. They were participants in one of the most famous home runs ever hit in New York, let alone baseball history. I was in awe that they were close friends, and that the event that catapulted their lives in two different directions could bring them close so many years later.

Just as a reminder, the "Shot Heard 'Round the World" is the term given to the game-winning home run hit in 1951 by New York Giants outfielder Bobby Thomson off Brooklyn Dodgers ace Ralph Branca at the Polo Grounds to win the National League pennant. As a result of the "shot," the Giants won the game 5–4, defeating the Dodgers in their best-of-three pennant playoff series, 2 games to 1. Thomson's home run erased the last of what had been a 13½-game deficit in the standings to their crosstown rivals in the final weeks of the season. The Giants wound up losing to the Yankees, but nobody remembers anything other than Thomson's home run.

Forty years later, these two amazing sports figures were about to gorge themselves on lobster. I noticed that the handsome Bobby Thomson had aged gracefully and looked like a winner, from his dress to the way he carried himself. Ralph Branca exuded the exact opposite.

Now I was driving a Buick for all of about two thousand yards to another iconic sports figure, Jack Nicklaus. As I pulled into the club driveway and began to turn into the clubhouse, I saw Nicklaus waiting with his golf bags.

I slowly pulled the car in front of him. I put it in park, and he walked around the front to get in. He wanted to get out of there without too many people seeing him. When I went to open the door for him, it fell off the car and onto the ground—right at the feet of Jack fucking Nicklaus.

The door wasn't hanging on. It wasn't even close to being on. It wasn't attached to the car by any stretch of the imagination. It came right off in my hands and lay on the ground between me and Jack. I started to laugh nervously. Here was the greatest golfer in the world standing a foot away from me, and the door to his car had just fallen off. Nobody knew what to do.

I apologized and then made a joke about it. I asked him if he wanted me to take the other door off, so both sides would match. Jack didn't laugh. "What I want is a fucking car to drive to the hotel in, and preferably one with doors. And I'd like it now."

The scenario was funny to me, but Jack didn't see the humor in it at first. I mean, of all the Buicks—and there were hundreds of them—the only one that lost its door was the one I drove to get Nicklaus in. I made another sarcastic remark about it, and then he cracked and became a human. As tourney execs went bonkers on their walkie-talkies to get Mr. Nicklaus a new car, stat, Jack leaned into me, pressed a folded twenty into my hand, winked, and said, "That's why I drive a Cadillac, kid."

Twenty bucks and a wink from the Golden Bear—not bad!

By that time, my boss had arrived at the scene to make sure one of his employees didn't fuck up, and also to make sure everything was still kosher. Both he and Jack talked to a club executive, and then Nicklaus drove off. I was about to run and get another car when my boss called me over to him.

He asked me what happened, and I told him the story. He gave me a big hug and said that Nicklaus had raved about how I handled it. He wanted to reward me. I figured there was a big cash payment coming my way, but no. Because of how I handled the situation, he wanted me to join a veritable Navy SEAL–type team of valet parkers for a special private house party in the Hamptons next weekend, with a major reward after working the event.

That Saturday, I met five other guys, all high school seniors, at the mall parking lot where we would get into one of the kids' conversion vans. Phillip was the driver, the boss sat shotgun, and then the rest of us hung in the back. We drove out to Southampton, and valet-parked a crazy wealthy house party until midnight. We each got four hundred dollars for the night, but the boss promised us an even bigger bonus. The best way to reward us, he figured, was to get all of us blowjobs from a New York City hooker. Oy vey, here we go again. I had been in this exact position the summer before with Steven and Mike. I was in a bad spot again. But I was stuck in the van and had no way of getting out of it.

We cruised Midtown for a hooker and again found one near an empty lot. Our boss negotiated with her for about ten minutes. When he was done, he ordered everybody out of the van and told us we would go one at a time. It was his treat. Seven guys and one woman with superhuman lips and jaw strength, I figured. My only goal was to try to delay as long as possible having to get in the van with her. The hooker he had picked could have been my last hooker's grandmother. She was a walking tragedy.

The group of us hung out behind the van in the corner of the parking lot, talking shit about what we were going to do when it was our turn, and joking about how badly the guy inside the van must be performing. One after the next, each one of these guys entered the van, and within ten minutes they exited with smiles wide as the moon. Some pathetic streetwalker had just blown them with a condom on.

I imagine these guys didn't get laid much, but back then neither did I. I just wasn't willing to be the eighth guy blown by a nasty hooker. I didn't want to be the first, either. The whole thing was disgusting to me, but for a teenage boy, if everybody else is doing it, you are in a weird spot if you say that you aren't. My mother used to ask whether I'd jump off a bridge if my friends did, and I'd tell her that I would go last and then just not do it.

This strategy worked well for me later in life. Two years ago, my wife and I were in South Florida for the Super Bowl with some friends. After a good, solid day of drinking, we all decided, "Let's get some tattoos." I'd often thought about getting one, but I'd always had a problem with what to get and where on my body to get it, not to mention its permanence. We walked into a random tattoo parlor and there were three people inside the store. One guy had bolts in his forehead—real bolts had been surgically embedded in his forehead. They stuck out like horns. The second guy had African hoops in his earlobes that extended past his chin. Two freaks. The third guy, the tattoo artist himself, greeted us chomping on takeout Chinese food. "What kind of fucking tattoo do you guys want?" he asked.

Okay, peace out. We walked out of the store, and luckily for us, there was another tattoo parlor a few doors down. There were no customers at all inside, which I suppose wasn't a good sign, but it was clean. Everyone decided this place was the best. My wife went first. She got the names of our kids written in script in between her toes. I noticed that the tattoo artist was shaking a lot throughout the procedure like he had Parkinson's. Maybe he was just nervous. When she showed me the finished product, the ink had bled so badly it looked like he threw on some green paint and she was rocking a nonsensical Philadelphia Eagles coloring on her toes.

My buddy's wife went next. She got a small heart tattoo with her kids' and husband's initials on her left butt cheek. I thought it came out well.

During the girls' tattoos, I wandered into a bar next door. For the first time in my life, I was thrilled to hear someone inside the bar yell, "Carton, what's up!" Now, you have to remember, it was midafternoon and a solid 80 degrees out, and I was inside a random bar in Fort Lauderdale. Turns out the only people in the bar are from New York, and they listen to my show on the radio.

"Let's do a shot!" they bellowed, and I was happy to oblige—so happy I bought four rounds of shots and five dozen wings, and spent more than an hour with the group.

By the time my buddy was up for his tattoo and I was supposed to be picking out mine, I was drunk. He asked me to help him pick out what to get and decided it was going on his ankle. He wavered back and forth from Chinese symbols to astrological signs to random drawings. He decided on Chinese or astrological. He asked me what I thought. I said, "How do you know what the Chinese symbol really is? For all you know, it means 'pussy' or 'fuck me' or 'kick the idiot.' Wouldn't that suck if that's the tattoo you wound up with?"

He decided on his astrological sign and showed it to the shaky-handed tattoo artist. As he did, the shaking got worse. I decided that was my out. Who could argue it? My wife had green shit on her toes, and my buddy's ankle was getting mauled by the needle. He wound up with what looks like a headless snake with his kids' and wife's initials on either side of it.

I chose to go last, and as a result I have no tattoo, which is a relief, considering what theirs look like.

Moments away from my turn with the hooker, I was hoping that the idea of going last would work out. There were two guys left before me. The boss was starting to get itchy. Not itchy because he got blown by a nasty hooker, but itchy because we had been in the lot a long time and he was pissed that he had paid her as much as he did.

He huddled us together and said, "Listen, when the last guy goes, I want all of you to get in the van right away." He was so agitated that he had lost track of who did and didn't go, and no one else seemed to care, either, once they had shot their loads. The guy before me got out of the van, and our boss looked around and said "Everybody go?" We all yelled, "Yup!" I was free and clear, but what happened next was one of the most ridiculous things I have ever seen. We all got in the van as instructed, and Phillip started the car. There were now eight guys in the back of a van with one hooker, and she knew something was fucked-up.

Looking nervous, she started to get dressed. As she stood up to get out, she was facing inside the van, holding her purse in one hand and the door handle in the other for balance as she tried to put on her high heel. Just then the boss grabbed one of those handlebars, drew his left foot backward, and with all his might kicked the hooker as hard as he could in the chest. He grabbed her pocketbook as she fell backward out of the van. He yelled for Phillip to hit the gas, and we pulled away.

It all happened in slow motion, and I can still see the woman flying out of the van. Before the door swung shut, she yelled, "Stop, you motherfuckers, you stole my makeup!" That seemed strange to me. She had to have gotten a few hundred dollars for blowing eight guys, and she was worried about her makeup?

My boss instructed Phillip to run every red light and get far away from the area. Nothing but dumb luck saved us from being shot at by a pimp, arrested by police, or something in between. When we got several blocks away, my boss opened her purse to retrieve his money, but the only things he found inside were lipstick and a roll of nickels that one of the guys gave her as a tip. ("Who carries rolls of nickels around?" is a good question. Another is, "Who tips hookers with it?") There was no money to be found.

This hooker was smarter than he thought. She rolled the money up and hid it on her body, just in case some douchebag decided to get his money back by karate-kicking her out of a van at one in the morning.

The whole way home, I kept thinking, fuck Jack Nicklaus. If he hadn't said anything to my boss, I would not have been an eyewitness to the drop-kicking of a hooker.

To this day, every time I see the Golden Bear, it makes me remember how he indirectly got me in front of a hooker.

Years later, when I was hosting a sports talk show in Cleveland, Ohio, a local golf club asked me to come out and see the progress of the new course they were building, which Jack Nicklaus was designing. They had the idea for me to sit in a golf cart next to Jack as he drove from hole to hole and pointed out what needed to be done, and how it would ultimately play. The course was still just razed land and dirt, and I announced to the half-dozen other folks that were going to join us on the drive that Jack and I were old friends. This was going to be a great reunion. The general manager of the club of course asked how we knew each other, and while Jack kind of grimaced like he had no idea, I reminded him of the car door falling off.

It would have been great if Jack did remember, but this was seven years later. It would have been even greater if Jack had played along by throwing out a simple "Oh yeah, that was you? Wow, great to see you again, boy! You've come a long way from parking cars." But all I got from Jack in front of the group was "Can we start the tour?"

I sat in the cart next to him, perturbed that he didn't remember. Why didn't he do the right thing, just guy to guy? But after a while I forgot about it, thrilled to witness Jack Nicklaus take us through each hole. On one hole there was a big weeping willow that they had not cut down, on Jack's orders. We stood on a hill of dirt and Jack said, "On this hole, you will use a five-iron off the tee." One of the club executives asked, "Why not a driver?" Jack said matter-of-factly, "Because if you use a driver, the tree will come into play—not now, but ten years from now when the course is more mature." Fucking awesome! He had contemplated club selection for a shot he couldn't even hit for ten years.

I had witnessed greatness. But he didn't remember the door incident, so I decided to get him back when we stopped for drinks about halfway through the tour. I said, "Come on, Jack, it's okay to tell the guys you remember. I mean, I remember the tip you gave me, five bucks. I was disappointed." Jack shot right back and said, "I gave you a twenty, and I heard your boss was giving you an even bigger bonus than that. Now is everybody ready to see the back nine?"

Long live the Golden Bear.

COCKROACHES AND OLD PEOPLE 16

It's funny, but when I was nineteen, I hated my WFAN internship. I did it in the summer of 1988, as the station celebrated its first anniversary. Back then, there was no guarantee that the station would make it, or be the success that it eventually was. It was doing terribly in the ratings and was on the verge of financial collapse.

I had been listening to WFAN at night. I was mesmerized by the fact that there were people talking about sports in a way I had never heard before. Prior to that, the only time I had ever heard anyone do sports talk was when Art Rust Jr. was a nighttime host at WABC. I would hear him if we happened to be in the car and my father had the Yankees game on. But WFAN was the first radio station I ever made it a point to listen to under the covers until late at night.

So I was thrilled when I got the internship at WFAN, but it turned out to be really boring, and it taught me nothing about being on the radio. I erased eight-track cassette tapes, sat in the production room during the Pete Franklin afternoon show, and counted the seconds until I could leave.

Few young people were there, unlike today, and the adults who ran the newsroom were serious about their craft. Every day, I questioned how in the world I would ever get a job in an environment like that— or be happy doing it. Everybody in the building seemed miserable, including the on-air host, Pete Franklin, whose show I was interning for. I never did another radio internship because of my WFAN experience, and it wasn't until they changed hosts and became a local radio station that I fell back in love with the station.

My first postcollege life-changing moment came in the summer of 1991, the year I graduated from Syracuse. I was teaching baseball at a camp in Naples, Maine, for the summer before I set out on my path toward getting a real job. The idea of never leaving camp was always in the back of my mind. Being a camp owner would be awesome, I thought, but I wasn't ready for it at that time.

I had done some broadcasting for the college radio station while I was at Syracuse, and figured I might as well give that a shot before I became a counselor for the rest of my life. Toward the end of my senior year, I made a demo tape of play-by-play basketball and sports talk, and began to send it out to various stations across the country. Today, I see entitled kids who think they should be on the air right away in a major market, but I was willing to go anywhere and do anything.

While a lot of people know what they want to do by the time they graduate from college, I knew only what I did *not* want to do. I knew that I would never work a nine-to-five job, and I knew that I could not wear a jacket and tie to work every day. I had enjoyed doing the college radio sports show, and I was a big fan of WFAN radio. While I dreamed about what it might be like to be a talk show host for a living, it wasn't as if that was the end-all for me. My passion for being in the bar/restaurant business was just as strong. As my college days came to an end, I figured it couldn't hurt to send out some of my demo tapes to see what would happen.

The first station that offered me a job was the only station that did, and it was based in Georgetown, Texas. A small *Friday Night Lights* kind of town, twenty miles outside Austin. When I got the call, I was told to hold on for the program director. After enduring a few minutes of country music, a Texas-sized bellow came across the phone. In his best country twang, the program director said, "Craig Carton, my name is Cowboy Otis, and I would love to have you come to our station." Cowboy Otis, what the fuck, I thought. He went on and on about how I would be covering high school football games and doing updates for the station, and that I would earn a $16,000 salary. I needed to be ready to start by July 1.

Was this my moment? I wondered. Would I start in Georgetown, Texas, and years later tell my kids how Cowboy Otis was the greatest guy in the world and like a second father to me, and I couldn't have made it to the network level if not for him?

No way. I decided that it wouldn't take long for Cowboy and his friends to dislike the Jewish kid from New York. I politely passed on the job. Without any other offers, I drove to Naples, Maine, to be a camp counselor. While there, I was summoned to the office one day in late July to take an important phone call. Normally an important phone call is not a good thing, but in this case it was.

My buddy Marc Bronitt was on the phone. Marc and I had been close friends since junior high school, and he went to Syracuse, too. He had sat in on my first college radio call-in show at 'Cuse. His mother was a radio personality at the legendary Z-100 in New York

City. Her name was Claire Bronitt, but she went by the name Claire Stevens on the air and was part of the Scott Shannon Morning Zoo. Marc told me that his mother was at the wedding of a radio friend in Buffalo. She just happened to be sitting at a table with the general manager of a station there. He told her that he was looking for a new sports talk person.

When radio people get together, all they talk about is radio. So I was lucky that she sat at his table and heard they needed a new employee. Marc gave me directions to send the tape of my college show and a cover letter referencing his mom's name to Chuck Finney, the program director at WGR in Buffalo. I did as I was told.

I gave my parents' phone number to Chuck with the explanation that if he liked my tape and wanted to talk, he could reach me through them as I was in Bumfuck, Maine, for the summer. My brother, Jeff, typed the letter, made the tape, and FedExed it to Finney the next day.

A week later, I was summoned again to the camp office for an important phone call. It was my brother telling me that Finney called and wanted me to call him to introduce myself. I called Chuck. He was gregarious over the phone. He told me a little bit about the station, and said that he liked my tape and that I should come to Buffalo. I packed up everything I owned into the 1980 Buick I was driving at the time and drove to Buffalo to start my professional life, or so I thought.

My moment was here. This would be a defining point in my life, but I didn't know it at the time. By getting the job in Buffalo, I would meet people who, twenty years later, still look out for my well-being, and I would be heard in a Top 35 market without even knowing it. I would wind up being promoted to a Top 6 market and have the chance to host the morning show in the country's biggest market. If I'd messed up and hadn't represented myself in the right manner—if the interview hadn't gone well—I never would have gotten into radio. I had no other leads, I only had one demo tape, and I didn't know much about the business.

I got to Buffalo late on a Sunday night and checked into a dumpy little motel. My meeting was Monday morning at nine. I woke up early the next day, put on a suit, and drove to the station. It was in what used to be a Victorian home, in a neighborhood of residential houses; homey and small-market, pre–consolidation of radio, for sure. I walked in and was introduced to Chuck. We spoke for about thirty minutes or so about what the station needed, what my experience was, all the normal Q&A stuff, and then he dropped the bomb on me.

"Craig, it was nice meeting you. We will let you know." What? I thought I had the job. Here was my moment. I could extend my hand and thank him for his time and walk out, or I could do something brash. I did the brash thing, but I did it without thinking. Only years later did I realize that this act changed my life. I said, "Chuck, when we spoke on the phone, you told me I had the job."

He replied, "I told you we liked you, but we have four other candidates that we're scheduled to interview." I said, "Listen, if you look out that window, you'll see a 1980 Buick loaded with all of my belongings, and that car isn't going to make it back to where I'm from. I promise I will never embarrass you in any way on or off the air. I don't do drugs, and I'm not an alcoholic. I need and want this job."

"I like your spunk, kid. You know what, that's the attitude we need around here. You're hired."

I was stunned, but went right into negotiation mode. "Chuck, it's time to talk money." He smiled and said "Okay, go ahead." I had it in my mind that I wanted to make $20,000 in my first real job, and I told him so. He said, "We will pay you twelve thousand," so I extended my hand and said, "Sixteen thousand it is," figuring we would split the difference.

Chuck said, "It's twelve thousand, kid. Two hundred and fifty dollars a week before taxes, take it or leave it. I'll give you the week to find a place to live, and you start next Monday."

We shook hands, and I went about finding an apartment.

Had I accepted his word that he had other people to interview and walked out that door, I never would have gotten that job. And I don't think I ever would have made a career in radio. Unless I was willing to go work for Cowboy Otis, I had no other options.

I set out to find a suitable place to live, which ain't easy on $250 a week, before taxes. After a few hours of looking all over suburban Buffalo, I stopped into a sports bar named Malone's on Delaware Avenue in Kenmore, a blue-collar, steel-mill-worker kind of town. While waiting for my wings to arrive, I drank a beer and looked out the window. I noticed a vacancy sign on the building across the street.

I finished my wings and a few more beers, and walked across the street to the decrepit six-story building, wondering if I had found a place to live. As it turned out, the building was an old-age home. Yes, they did have a vacancy, but for someone much older than me. I told the manager of the building that I didn't think I would be there long, I didn't do drugs, and I wasn't a big drinker. Hey, two out of three facts ain't bad. I added that I would help the elderly with their groceries and help him shovel. He agreed on a handshake, and told me the monthly rent would be $99. A hundred bucks for a studio apartment infested with cockroaches and surrounded by old people. I was in heaven! I moved in that day. Two days later on August 24, 1991, I started at WGR Radio in Buffalo New York. My life would never be the same.

RADIO RAT 17

It's hard for the average person to understand the social life of a celebrity. To make tons of money, to have women throwing themselves at you night and day. No matter how good you look and no matter how much money you might make, even if you're a lawyer or a successful businessperson, you need to work to get laid. You may not have to work as hard as a bus driver, but you can't walk into a bar and expect women to throw themselves at you. While I can't relate to Alex Rodriguez or Derek Jeter by any stretch, when you are on the radio in a given market, you become a local celebrity—and for some women, thankfully, that's all you need to be.

I had been in Buffalo for about three months when I realized the power of being "famous." By no means was I famous, but I had built a loyal following on the air. When I first started there, I did six-hour

shifts alone on Saturday and Sunday, and during the week I produced the John Otto nighttime show, and I also did as much work as I could during the day. I was a radio rat. I wanted to learn it all, and the only way to do it was to be there every day, all day, to see what the business was all about and figure out what I could do, and do well. (Plus, on $250 a week, I couldn't afford to do much outside of work, anyway.)

Being the new blood in town and not being from Buffalo had its benefits among the ladies. Most of them were depressed at the prospect of winding up with a loser from Buffalo with no future. I was fresh meat to them, and I had decided I would be lowering my standards while I was there—not because I was Don Juan, but because I'd gotten used to some real lookers at Syracuse.

The first girl to show me any real attention was a gal named Michelle. She was a dwarf who I met out one night. I had never seen a dwarf before, let alone have her talk the dirtiest sex talk I have ever heard to this day in my life.

When I saw her, she didn't pay me any attention, but soon thereafter, she learned that I was the guy she had been listening to on the radio. Michelle offered to do things to me that I had never considered before or since. I would love to tell you that I took advantage of this situation and had unbelievable dwarf sex, but I didn't. I did, however, tell her that she could do some things to herself and videotape them for me. Not only did she oblige by telling me what she did and how she did it, but had the Internet been around in 1991, she would have been its first star.

Without getting into too many details, she was willing to role-play an XXX-rated scene right out of *The Wizard of Oz*, and another as an Oompa-Loompa from *Charlie and the Chocolate Factory*. Even today when I see those movies with my kids, the phrase "We welcome you to Munchkin Land" has a different meaning. Augustus Gloop drinking out of the chocolate river and being tended to by six Oompa-Loompas gives me the chills.

Having turned down Michelle, I was still single and enjoying the limited nightlife in Buffalo. It wasn't limited because there was a lack of bars. But if you weren't a Buffalo Bill or if your name wasn't Jim Kelly or one of his brothers, you had to go on a search-and-destroy mission akin to SEAL Team 6 finding Osama bin Laden. Or host a popular AM sports show and hang out at the same bar as often as possible so that everyone there knew who you were. I hung out at a bar called Jovi's, also on Delaware Avenue, a few blocks from my apartment. I met a waitress there and asked her out. We agreed to meet at Jovi's to have some drinks on the house first. She was nineteen and not legal, but they let her drink there. They all knew me by this time, so I had a house account and paid it off with tickets to Bills games and Sabres games that I got from the station.

The date started great. We did a few shots and drank beers, and she told me she wanted to take me to a cool spot in Buffalo. We drove for about twenty minutes and approached the entrance to a public park. She directed me to an exact spot where we could stop. I parked the car, left the battery on, and turned on the radio. And then she jumped me. She was hot, and it seemed like this was going to be an amazing experience. Just as we got our clothes off, I heard a knock on the window that scared me so much I popped up and hit my head on the ceiling of the car. Holy shit, a flashlight shone into the window and a voice said, "Lower your window, son." It was a police officer.

Not only had I had a few drinks and drove to the park, but my date was nineteen and she was bordering on drunk, too. The officer told me the park was closed and I was there illegally. Woo-hoo, strike three, I thought. He asked me for my license and registration and then pointed the light toward my date. Fuck, I thought, here we go: Were you drinking? and then some.

Instead, I heard these words:

"Suzy, is that you?"

"It's me, Bob."

"Haven't I told you to stop bringing guys here after hours?"

She started small-talking him. They grew up together, and banging guys in cars in this exact spot in this park was her m.o. God knows how many guys she had done this with, not that I cared. I was just happy to get out of there. But my night wasn't over yet.

Suzy had kept saying to me that no matter when the date ended, I had to be sure to escort her to the door of her house. I reassured her twenty-five times that I would, and that it wasn't a problem. I couldn't understand why she kept making it such an issue. We arrived at her house around four in the morning. As I put the car in park, she again said, "Now you have to walk me to the door." I said that I would. As we walked from the driveway to the house, I noticed that it looked as if all the lights were on inside.

I wasn't sure if I was going to be shot by her dad for keeping her out so late, or what, but I sucked it up, held her hand, and walked her to the front door. When she opened it, about twenty people jumped out and said, "Surprise!" This startled me. Was there a birthday? Not that I knew of. But no, the surprise was for me.

She had told her family that the guy they listened to on the radio has asked her out. This was a big deal to them. They sent her out on a date with me, and then invited all of their relatives over to the house to wait for me to bring her back in whatever condition so that they could meet me, talk sports with me, and feed me. I met every cousin, uncle, and nephew the girl had, and ate one of the greatest meals of my life.

I didn't roll out of there until almost seven in the morning. I realized that "celebrity" could be great, but also dangerous.

It wasn't until I got to Philadelphia that I learned just how dangerous. But that's a later story.

The best example of the dangers of celebrity is Alex Rodriguez, the star third baseman for the New York Yankees. Married to his high school sweetheart and the father of adorable girls, Alex, along with the rest of New York, woke up to the following headline: ALEX RODRIGUEZ BUSTED WITH BLONDE AT TORONTO STRIP CLUB. It was the single biggest story of the year and was talked about for months and months. Every day, thousands of your friends who travel on business wind up going to strip clubs, hiring hookers, or picking up random women at hotel lobby bars. None of them get caught. None of their wives or girlfriends have any idea. And of course none of them are famous.

There are more than 1.4 million entries on Google that come up when you search for "Alex Rodriguez Strippers." The end result was Alex's wife wearing a T-shirt to a Yankees home game that said "FU" on the back collar. Sadly, shortly after that they got divorced. So sure, celebrity sounds glamorous compared to our lives—most of it is—but the next time you do something a little left or right of center, imagine TMZ there waiting to catch you.

ONE LAP DANCE OVER THE TOP

18

I had been in Buffalo for six months when it happened for the first time. I walked into the station and the main secretary told me there was a message for me. I didn't have a phone extension there, and to my knowledge nobody had ever called for me at the main switchboard. This was something entirely new. The message slip said that some guy named David George had called, and please call him back ASAP. I went to a cubicle and dialed.

The phone rang twice, and then a pleasant-sounding woman answered. "Three W-EEEE, may I help you?" I didn't know what "Three W-EEEE" was, so I said, "May I please talk to David George?" still having no idea who he was. David picked up right away and said hello, and told me he was a big fan. I thanked him, and he referenced a radio bit I had done the weekend before and laughed out loud. Clearly a

smoker, David's laugh was more half-cough. When he finished re-counting the radio moment, he told me that he was the program direc-tor of WWWE Radio in Cleveland, Ohio, a legendary radio station with a signal that reached twenty-eight states and half of Canada, at least according to their own promotions. I assumed the Canadian part was a fib, but shit, this station was big-time.

David told me that the signal from Buffalo made a straight shot to Cleveland during the day, and he had become a big fan of my weekend marathon solo shows. It just went to show, every time you went on the air, you had no idea who might be listening. If you ever showed up unprepared, you never knew what future opportunity you might be blowing.

David told me that he wanted me to come to Cleveland to inter-view to become their new permanent nighttime host. Shocked and excited, and surprisingly aroused, I almost shouted out loud like I was starring in a bad porn film with Nina Hartley. I took the day off from work and drove my Buick to Cleveland. They had made a reservation for me in a downtown hotel, and I was told to be in the lobby bar at 6 p.m. to meet David and other executives from the radio station.

When I walked in there, only three people were at the bar. Two of them were dressed as if they came right from an IBM meeting: dark suits, white shirts with tons of starch, and an uneasy look about them. And then there was David George. He had stubby fingers, wore a suit a full size too big, and had lousy shoes on, but he was warm and welcoming. He said with his smoker's cough, "There's my guy, Craig Carton. Great to meet you."

He introduced me to his colleagues: David Popovich, who was the operations manager, and Roger Turner, the grand poobah and general manager. David was engaging, but Roger, who had to be in his late fif-ties or early sixties, was standoffish. We ordered drinks. I didn't know that I was about to go on an eight-hour interview, the longest of my life.

They dove in with basic background questions, and then the GM, who made little eye contact and seemed disinterested, asked, "What is your radio philosophy?" Hmmm . . . . I had been in radio for five months, and I had no philosophy about radio, but I did know how to bullshit. I had sized him up as soon as I walked in the room as an older conservative who demanded respect. I gave it a shot.

"My philosophy is to respect the audience and relate to them, so that whenever they turn on your great radio station, they feel like they are listening to a friend." Such bullshit, but I figured he would eat it up. He didn't respond, and uncomfortably I waited until one of the two Davids jumped in with their next question.

We had spent about forty-five minutes and three cocktails in the hotel lobby bar when Roger got up and said, "You boys are going to dinner, right?" They nodded, and he said, "Not me. Nice meeting you, Craig. Have a good night," and he was gone. The three of us finished our drinks, got into a waiting car, and drove to an Italian restaurant.

Over the course of the next two hours, we finished off three bottles of red wine and engaged in some mindless banter. I was more than buzzed, as were they, and our conversation had gotten louder and louder, and less and less formal. At some point during dessert, David George said, "We ought to show him the station; it's right around the corner." The three of us stumbled out of the restaurant and walked two blocks to the station, which sat at the top of a high-rise building in downtown Cleveland, overlooking the Flats.

As the elevator door opened onto the floor, they remembered that the guy I would be replacing was on the air at this exact time. Radio guys don't give a fuck how they treat employees, especially once they have given up on them. The rub here was that the guy I was replacing wasn't being fired. He was being reassigned to be my update guy, which was a comeuppance. He had been on the air in that market for twenty years, was well liked, and was a nice guy. Problem was, he was boring, and nobody was listening to his show.

The two Davids didn't want him to see me, but in the event he did, they concocted a story that I was a nephew just in town who wanted to see the station. They couldn't be that dumb, but they were. It never occurred to them what would happen if they told that story and thirty days later, I was back to host the show.

The guy never saw me, and we got in and out without being noticed by anyone. The station was impressive and had all the trimmings, in direct contrast with Buffalo. We left the building and hit a pool hall, and we had a few shots and more drinks. I was flat-out trashed. They were, too. They suggested hitting a strip club next.

I was drunk, but I was alert enough to know that. I was trying my hardest not to do anything stupid. These guys either didn't get out much, or they knew how to convince someone to come to work for them. There is nothing more awkward than getting a lap dance while a guy almost old enough to be your dad pays for it and sits next to you watching it. Yet that's what happened. A few lap dances, more shots, and after what turned out to be eight hours, they declared the night over and drove me back to my hotel.

On the way, I summoned up the courage to ask the guys about salary and length of contract. When I did, Dave Popovich, who was sitting shotgun, turned around and deadpanned me eyeball-to-eyeball. "Nice meeting you. The night is over; goodbye," he said. Wow, my spirits sank. I figured if they didn't want me, they would have dumped me after dinner. I said, "Don't you think we should have a quick chat about the ballpark you're in for this job?" and again he gave me steely eyes and said, "Good night." I went to bed miserable. Not only had

I had to watch a forty-year-old guy get a lap dance, but I might have gotten shot down for the job.

My hotel phone rang early the next morning. It was David George. He said it was great to meet me, and they had decided after their morning meeting that I was their guy. They were going to FedEx me an offer. I asked him what the offer was. He refused to tell me, other than it would be FedExed over. Strange, for sure. Two days later, the offer came to my roach-infested retirement-home studio apartment. They had offered me a three-year deal with base salaries of $30,000, $31,000, and $32,000. Nothing to negotiate. I signed on the dotted line. I had just tripled my salary in less than a year.

In the year I spent in Cleveland, David George quit to run a newspaper stand outside a popular mall. Jay Clark, a well-thought-of programmer from New York City, replaced him. Imagine leaving an executive-level job in radio to sell twenty-five-cent newspapers out-doors, seven days a week. Radio seems glamorous, but for most people not only is it not glamorous, it means a low-paying, insecure profes-sional life. Yet it is so addicting that most people stay—or they have no other skills, so they're unhireable anywhere else.

Jay and I got along right away. He seemed to like me. He invited me over to his apartment to eat dinner with his son several times, which is why I was so shocked at what happened in March 1993.

I had already been on the receiving end of several performance-related memos from Roger Turner, the GM. Roger spent forty-five minutes with me the night of my interview, and he had me into his office on the first day of work. From that point to this one, I never saw the man, not a single time. Roger was a pussy, afraid of looking another guy in the face. He feared real conversation. I grew up without much real face-to-face contact with my dad, but that Roger communi-cated with me by memos was new.

The Indians were still a bad team when I first got to Cleveland. I took them to task almost every night—not the players specifically, but the ownership. One night Roger was at a black-tie event with Dick Jacobs, the team's owner, and he received an earful from Jacobs about "the new punk kid" on his radio station who was calling him names. I called him "Arthur," a reference to the movie character played by Dudley Moore. My point was that Jacobs was an incompetent owner. That point was heard loud and clear.

I had become close with some of the young players on the Indians. I was twenty-two years old and had been in radio for all of seven months. At the time, WWWE Radio was a conservative talk station with a syndicated Rush Limbaugh as its main attraction. I arrived as a loud-mouthed kid from New York who didn't hide the fact that he thought Cleveland sports was a joke, and I was right. The only winning team they had was the Cavaliers, which could never get past Michael Jordan and the Bulls. The Browns were being led by a young, unproven head coach named Bill Belichick and had no chance of winning with Todd Philcox as the replacement quarterback for Bernie Kosar.

Then came the Indians, the true joke of Cleveland. By the time I arrived, however, there was a change brewing. The Indians traded Joe Carter for two no-name players who turned out to be Carlos Baerga and Sandy Alomar. Later the organization was selected as Organization of the Year by *Baseball America*. While the Indians were going to be a team on the rise, the rest of the Cleveland sports scene was much more complicated. The Cavaliers were a perennial playoff team, and if not for Jordan, they most certainly would have gone to an NBA Final. They were loaded with Brad Daugherty, Mark Price, Craig Ehlo, and many more. The town wasn't as rabid about the Cavs as they were the Browns, but this team was perfect for blue-collar Cleveland as they were led by a hardworking, overachieving white point guard in

Price. He was religious. He never went out socially, never showboated, couldn't dunk, and he was slow. But boy, could he play—and play like an all-star, which he was.

Cleveland sports fans hated Jordan because he always stood in their way of playoff success. I decided one day to take advantage of that hatred. I announced on-air that I would give all listeners a chance at a free shot at Jordan. I bought a life-sized cardboard cutout of MJ and tied it to a parking lot pole. I invited fans to throw their choice of rocks, apples, and other assorted fruits at the cutout. Fans waited in line for an hour to get their shot.

Cleveland was and will always be a Browns football town. Coach Bill Belichick would go on to win three Super Bowls with the Patriots and appear in two more, both losses to the New York Giants. Many consider him the best coach of his generation, and rightfully so. In Cleveland he is known as the guy who benched local legend Bernie Kosar for unknown Todd Philcox. He also had a losing record while there.

I had season tickets in the Dawg Pound, the most raucous seats in the entire Municipal Stadium; end-zone seats with the most ardent of Browns fans. In addition to attending the games, I also became close with Bill. So close that one day when we were talking with each other, he asked me if I had any interest in working for an NFL team. The thought had never occurred to me, but he explained how he would be willing to tutor me. He knew I wasn't thrilled about my general manager at the radio station, and he offered me the job of unpaid intern with the promise of earning a small salary.

I was only making $30,000, so leaving radio for a low-paying job wouldn't change much for me. I told Bill I would think about it. He gave me a weekend to decide. When I turned the job down to pursue radio and give it everything I could, as I explained to him, he wound up finding someone else to take it. The man who ultimately took the job was a guy named Eric Mangini. Fifteen years later he became the New York Jets head coach, and then the Browns head coach. He now works for ESPN. Of course, my thought was, I could have been the New York Jets head coach!

During the spring of 1992, I became friends with Charles Nagy, who was becoming the ace of the Cleveland Indians staff, as well as a number of other players on the team. We weren't friends in the sense that we all had each other's phone numbers, but we worked out in the same gym, partied at the same clubs, and knew each other. One player once came to my rescue at a sports bar when Sandy Alomar came after me to protest some things I had said about him on my radio show.

One day the Indians had an afternoon at home, and I was off that night, so I figured I'd grab some beers and take in a ball game at Cleveland's old Municipal Stadium. Armed with a press pass, I thought I'd hit the dugout before the game and say hello to some of the guys. When I got there, the guys started egging each other on to "Show him! Show him!" I had no idea what they were talking about. I just hoped that I was not about to be on the receiving end of some sort of medieval sexual initiation.

Once I was assured that I was safe, I relented and asked what they wanted me to see. Like a bunch of giggling schoolgirls, they all followed as one of the players led me into the trainer's room. After one final warning to me about not revealing on my show what I was about to see, I opened the door to what was the inner sanctum of any locker room, and heard a constant banging.

Bang bang bang bang!

About fifteen feet in front of me there was a player sitting on one of those old swivel stools you'd see in a doctor's office. He had a practice jersey on as well as his stirrup socks, and his pants were around his ankles. It was a fellow player, and the guys behind me tried to stifle their laughs as I peered closer so that I could see what the deal was . . .

The deal was both frightening and amazing. The player was one of the young stars on the team, and part of the Indians' future success. But on this day, a few hours before game time, he sat in that swivel chair with his back to the door. He had his cock in the palm of his hand, and he was holding it and slamming it as hard as he could against the stool. Bang, bang, bang! He didn't stop.

I wondered if he had a rhythm to the banging, or if he did it for a certain number of times or seconds, but the guys just told me he did it until he felt "right." I was dumbfounded, yet couldn't turn away from the sight of a grown man slamming his dick as hard as he could against anything, let alone a stool. When I finally turned around, the guys broke into uproarious laughter that didn't stop until we left the clubhouse. To his credit, the player never flinched, never acknowledged my presence, and—coincidentally or not—went on to have a great year.

That visit may have been my first introduction to locker room antics, but over the course of the next twenty years, I became privy to some good ones. The locker room can be an intimidating place. No, I'm not just talking about walking into a professional locker room where guys are hung like mules. Sometimes you can mistake a dude's cock for a jump rope. I once saw three kids playing double Dutch with an NFL star's junk. Okay, that's a lie, but they could have. It was enormous and impressive, and I stared at it for far too long.

For most of us, the first locker room experience you have is with your father at a country club, YMCA, or other gym. There is nothing more frightening than the first time you see your own father and six of his buddies sporting full frontal, going for a steam. It's life-altering. Shriveled-up ball sacks, bellies hanging over their junk, saddle bags and pockmarked butt cheeks. It's enough to scare you into never taking your clothes off again.

Once you get through that nightmare, junior high school rolls around. The prospects of the communal shower confront you. Reputations are made in split seconds when you're a teenager and walking into the shower for the first time. If you're like me, and you're a grower and not a show-er, the shower experience is a tough one. You certainly don't want to get the reputation for having an inny, because then your lifelong prospects for pussy dwindle and you have to wait until you go to college to start with a fresh rap. Don't ever believe that chicks don't gossip. All it takes is one guy to tell his girlfriend that you have no dick, and before lunch the next day, you have no shot for a prom date unless you import her from Guam.

You also do not want to get caught stroking the junk to make it grow, because then you will be labeled a pervert. While there's nothing wrong with that, life ain't like *Glee,* and it's a tough existence at that age.

Imagine having a full-on boner when you walk into a communal shower area. This is the first place any of us will be seen naked by our peers, unless of course you were caught selling home Skype movies to neighborhood moms. If you have a full-on erection, a risk from rubbing it too much pre-shower, you'll be lucky not to get punched in the mouth.

Here are the rules of the communal shower:

Wrap yourself with a towel and pretend you have to pee before going to the shower. Slap that little soldier of yours back and forth a bit, just to get the blood flowing and start the semi process. The semi, for those of you who haven't heard the term before, is when you're in between a full-on erection and totally soft. It's pleasurable, too, and as I mentioned, one that I first learned during elementary gym class while climbing the rope.

As soon as you have a semi, get to the shower. Now when you take the shower, you're going to look straight ahead at the wall at all times, but as you walk in and take the towel off, every other dude will size you up, just as you will do to them. You'll look big, and that's all they will remember, since cock size and bench-press ability are the two most important ways we compare ourselves at that age.

When you return from the shower, I suggest putting your underwear on under the towel. Your excuse can be that in such close proximity, you don't need to risk an awkward accidental touching of your junk against a buddy's leg. So sit down on the locker room bench and put the underwear on, and then lose the towel.

Oh, I almost forgot: the one thing you never want to do is play a game of rattail and snap your towel against another dude's naked ass—ever, at any age, in any setting.

But I digress. Back to the black-tie event when Roger ran into Dick Jacobs, the Indians' owner. I doubt Roger ever listened to my show, but he was shocked by Jacobs complaining about me in front of the nose-in-the-air society of Cleveland. The next day he fired off a memo telling me to cease and desist from calling Jacobs "Arthur." I had to call him "Mr. Jacobs" from now on. A few other names were listed there as well. I was not allowed to refer to the Indians owner as a "butthead" and "loser," either.

I did what any thoughtful radio host who had just taken his time slot from twelfth in the ratings to fourth in only six months would do. I read the memo on the air, and then I reread it. This was a turning point in my relationship with the audience: it was real, it was relatable, and the fan base loved it. I was one of them now, and I was "so important" that the owner of the Indians himself had reacted to what I was saying.

Roger hated what I did, but again, rather than speak to me directly, he sent me yet another memo. What did he think I was going to do? This memo was threatening: "If you read this memo on the air, it will be construed as a disobeying a direct order from a superior, and as such may result in termination."

Hmmm . . . My show was on fire; ratings had never been higher for the time slot. I had been asked to do pregame and postgame shows for Cavalier basketball games to help their ratings. I felt untouchable.

I read the memo on the air.

When I came in the next day, I was expecting something, but all I got from Jay Clark was "Good show last night." Nothing else until the following Monday. I had put in for a few vacation days to go golfing in Myrtle Beach with Chris Beldotti, my best friend from college.

Working nights presented me with the opportunity to stroll throughout the building without interference. Only my update guy, my producer, and I were in the building after business hours. I strolled past the executive secretary's desk and happened to see my name on a piece of paper, so I investigated what it was. Turns out it was my vacation request form, and written on it in pencil was a handwritten note from Roger that stated, "No reason to approve this request. The plan we discussed will be in effect before these dates."

Motherfucker. I was going to be fired, and this coward didn't even have the balls to come and talk to me. I was livid. My sole focus became to torch Roger, which I did mercilessly on the show that night. I buried him without referencing the note I had seen. I didn't want them to know that I knew.

The next day I went to work early. I got there before noon, stormed into Jay Clark's office, and yelled, "What the fuck, you're firing me and you didn't have the common courtesy to say something?" I went on for a good minute or two, using every possible use of the word *fuck*.

Jay allowed me to rant, and then smirked and said, "Are you done?"

"I'm just getting started," I told him.

"Well, save your breath and sit down."

"I'd rather stand."

"Sit down and relax. You're not being fired, exactly."

"What the fuck does that mean?"

He said something I imagine nobody who has ever been fired has heard before. "We got you a job in Philly. You're going to be in a Top-Ten market."

"Ha-ha, yeah, right," I said. He went on to explain that yes, Roger wanted me fired. He'd wanted me out of the building ever since I read his memo on the air, but Dave Popovich was a big fan and was proud of what I had accomplished. Dave got Roger to delay the firing while Dave got in touch with a guy named Tom Bigby, who had started a new sports talk format in Philly on WIP Radio. Tom needed a new host, and my show fit his needs perfectly. Popovich and Bigby went back a decade, and on Dave's recommendation alone, Bigby wanted to bring me in. "Your last show here is the day before your vacation, and in the meantime, you will go to Philly and get together with Tom about your new gig. Congratulations!"

Holy shit, I thought, Philly? I was going back to the East Coast to be in a Top 10 market, and I still had no idea what the fuck I was doing. I left Cleveland for vacation and then Philadelphia, and never saw Roger again—but I did send him a memo before I left.

Roger,

Thanks for the opportunity to come to Cleveland. It's a wonderful town with amazing people.
Fuck you.

Regards,
Craig Carton

ROOM SERVICE, WITH A LITTLE EXTRA

19

I got to Philadelphia in the spring of 1993, just as WIP Radio was about to become a legend in radio circles. It was a small-powered station that had captivated the heart of Philadelphia with its take-no-prisoners guy talk, mixed in with hard-core sports passion. No X's and O's were discussed; no basketball or hockey debated. This was a radio station for Eagles fans, and almost exclusively for men. The station was being led by a guy named Angelo Cataldi, who had made his bones as an investigative reporter but took to radio for the better pay. He had figured out radio: be consistent, be entertaining, and give people what they want. What the people wanted was hot chicks, football talk, and nothing else.

The station was created by a behemoth of a man named Tom Bigby. I hadn't officially been in radio until I worked for Bigby. He

represented every typical quality of a radio programmer or boss. He thought he was bigger than the station. He thought he could turn anyone into a star. And he thought he knew everything about anything. He was right on all counts.

When the guys at Cleveland first set me up with Bigby, it was over the phone, and I thought he seemed pleasant enough. He spoke with a Louisiana drawl, and he was receptive to me. Before my new job was finalized, I had to fly in and do two weekend shifts for him so he could hear how I sounded on his station. I met with him on a rainy Friday, and he was the most intimidating guy I had ever seen. He weighed about four hundred pounds, and had small forearms. Wanting to prove to me right away that he was the boss, he told me to sit in and watch his afternoon show with Mike Missanelli and Steve Fredericks.

For my money, this was the single best show WIP ever had during my time there. Mike is a smart guy. He played college baseball, graduated from law school, and had an ego the size of Philly. He was partnered with Philly icon Steve Fredericks. They called their show *S&M* and it was the type of show I later patterned my own career after. Mike was a younger, more energetic guy, and Steve played his foil and the older-brother type. The only issue was that Steve could never win an argument, and could never call anybody out, because years earlier when he was the singular voice of Philadelphia sports on the radio, he was caught in a North Philly drug den with a shitload of heroin. He garnered the front page for it.

Both guys were pleasant to me, and Mike even said he was glad the station was bringing in some new young talent. To this day, he is the only guy who has ever welcomed me to the fraternity of on-air talent without fear that I was there to take his place. Mike and I got along great. Steve was receptive to me as well, and while we were never as close as Mike and I got, merely due to the age difference and because Steve wasn't socializing publicly anymore, we got along great from the first time we met.

About an hour into their show, Bigby came into the studio and ripped into Steve for something innocuous he'd said. Steve didn't say a word. He just gave him a look like, "Are you out of your mind?" and let Bigby blow his horn. It was obvious to all of us that Bigby had manufactured his disdain to show everyone, including the new guy, who was the boss. I got the message. Bigby was showing me that it was his station, and just in case I didn't get it, he pointed a few things out to me before I left for the day.

Inside the studio he had placed a box with three lights and a timer on it. This timer told you when to dump a caller. Tom believed that no caller should ever go more than two minutes, and even that was too long. When a caller came on the line, the green light lit up when the timer hit thirty seconds; a yellow light lit up warning you that the caller was now getting dangerously close to being on the air too long. When the timer hit ninety seconds, the light hit red. And if a caller ever hit two minutes, all the lights went nuts.

Tom took me to his office and showed me that not only did he have the same box with lights in his office, but in fact he could push a button himself and disconnect a caller, and he made it clear to me that he was always listening. He claimed he had the same setup in his house, but I never bought that. He did, however, have one more contraption, and that was a special phone line hooked into the studio that only he could dial. When he called that number, the phone lines blinked green and a strobe light went off, so you always knew when he was calling. Every show you did, you did it with him in mind. He was ruthless, maniacal, and a genius at the same time. You could never even think of letting a caller go overtime, or of sleepwalking through a segment.

Needless to say, I was a little nervous for my two tryout shows. Nobody had ever actually taught me how to do radio, and I had been in the profession for less than two years. Yet here I was, two tryouts away from landing a gig as the youngest full-time on-air sports talk host in America in a Top 20 market.

The first show I ever did was with a likable guy named Tom Sredenschek, a Fox producer who wanted to do radio. He was a nice guy, and he had been ordered to allow me to do the radio formatics, meaning I would introduce the callers, go to the commercial breaks, and so on. The four hours went by in a blur, and I was thankful that he was my first-ever partner. We did it again the next day, and again it felt smooth. Bigby never called during either show, and I had no plans to meet with him, because my flight back to Cleveland was the next morning. I called his office and left a message thanking him for the opportunity, and saying that I looked forward to chatting on Monday.

Bigby called Monday morning. He told me he hadn't heard either show, but he wanted to know what I thought. I told him that Tom Sredenschek was a good guy, it felt good being on Bigby's radio station, and I was eager to get started. He shot back that the shows were all right but I had let the callers talk too much. Not only had he listened, but he went on to critique specific calls at specific times. He also told me I should have smacked Tom several times because he was getting in the way of good radio. No response from me.

Bigby said that he wanted me to do nights and some weekends, and that he was prepared to make me an offer. Now remember, I started out making $12,000 living in a retirement home on August 24, 1991. On April 1, 1992, I signed a three-year contract making $30,000 per year. Now, in the spring of 1993, I was about to get an offer from Tom Bigby and WIP, just as it was about to hit the big time and become a legendary station.

Bigby asked me how much I would like to make. I assumed I would make more than I was making in Cleveland, but I had no idea what it would be, so I figured I'd take a shot. I threw out a crazy number and said $50,000. Tom came back with "How about I do you one better and pay you $52,500, and we call it a day?"

I said "yes" faster than an IHOP waitress agrees to blow Tiger Woods.

That was it. I would start May 1, 1993, and I would make $52,500. I only later learned that WIP was a union station, and that the union had negotiated that the minimum salary a full-time talk show host could make was $52,500. Bigby played with me and made it seem like he was doing me a favor. I bought it, but even after I found out, I didn't care one bit. I had more than quadrupled my salary in less than two years, and I was now in the sixth-biggest market in America.

I did the night show with a former Eagle named Garry "G" Cobb, and I also did an occasional weekend shift. Garry and I had a blast doing nights together and created a strong following. I loved Garry and still do, even though time and my failure to stay in touch with people have caused us to drift apart. Garry wasn't the best talk show host but he was always a solid friend and a great partner.

Working with G Cobb was great. He always had my back and always looked out for me, whether by bringing me on his weekly TV show, *G Cobb Live,* or taking me out to meet girls. G and I were very tight. During one show, G fell asleep. He was tired from running around all day, and he fell asleep on the air. It had happened before, but this time in particular he was out cold. The snoring was loud enough that you could hear it on the show. I elbowed him several times to wake him up, but no luck. We had a caller on the air who wanted Garry's perspective on some Flyers hockey issue. I elbowed G again pretty hard, and he popped up and for no reason at all, said,

"Randall Cunningham." I could barely contain my laughter, but I did long enough to say, "G, the caller asked you a question about the Flyers." Garry responded without missing a beat. "I know, Craig. Randall could have played hockey. He's a great athlete." I always laugh when I think back to that moment and all the good times I had with G.

G Cobb was a businessman and a hustler. I loved that about him. In addition to his TV show, he had business deals throughout the community. He worked hard at everything but radio. I believe it got to a point where Garry recognized that I prepared extensively for the show, and he knew he could count on me.

There came a time in WIP's history when we were not allowed to talk about so many sports topics. An edict came down from Bigby, and the whole radio station became guys doing top-ten lists. Bigby didn't believe there was a big enough audience for talking hockey, baseball after 1993, or Sixers hoops ever. That left one sport: Eagles all the time, or lists that guys would create to help get callers and make it through a show.

I hated the lists. I thought I could entertain listeners without them and without the calls, but there was nobody better at creating lists than G Cobb. His most popular list show was the famous "Ugly Show." Twice a year he would come on the air and say, "Craig, who is the ugliest guy in the public eye?" and bang, we would have at it. Four hours of me, Garry, and the callers just burying people for everything from looks, dress, to you-name-it.

During my first-ever Ugly Show, I nominated a guy named Larry Rosen. At the time, Spectacor was Philly's main sports cable supplier. Owned by the Sixers, it was the home of Sixers and Flyers broadcasts, and the precursor to Comcast Sports. Larry Rosen was its "star," for lack of a better description. He hosted all the pregame and postgame shows and was a major presence on the network. Coming from New

York and then even Buffalo and Cleveland, I had never seen a guy so ugly working full-time on television. I said so on the radio. I got the usual laughs and moved on, thinking nothing of it.

Tom Bigby was a lunatic, and every bit as powerful as the station he created. He considered himself a superstar, and acted as such. Once when I was traveling with the Eagles for a playoff game in Dallas against the Cowboys, Tom wanted me to do a three-hour show on the Saturday before the game. The only problem was, he never set up a radio station for me to broadcast from, so I had to do the whole show from the phone in my hotel room.

The show was minutes from starting. I asked the hotel to put a "Do Not Disturb" note on my room phone and dialed in to the radio station. There would be a cohost in the studio to help take calls, and I would host from my bed, essentially. Just as we went on-air, there was a knock on my door and the muffled sounds of someone saying, "Room service." I hadn't ordered any room service, so I ignored the knock and started the show.

"Live from the Hilton in Dallas . . ." Knock, knock. Again, "Room service . . ."

I reached over to the door with the phone in one hand. I opened it and in came Tom Bigby. He sat down on the bed and just stared at me while I tried to start the show. After a few minutes he gave me the sign to wrap up the segment and take a break. The whole time he never moved from my bed.

When he finally got up from the bed, he looked me in the eye. The smile disappeared. "Remember this: I am the star of WIP, and nobody else."

O-kay, got it, Tom. He was right. We all hated him, but every one of us who worked for him and had success has always pointed out that without Tom's insight and direction, none of us ever would have gotten as far as we did. Tom taught me that callers should be treated in the same way music stations use songs—only the best songs should ever make the air. Callers should take the conversation to another level. They should be entertaining; they should bring out the best in the host, and you should never take a call just for the sake of taking a call. Less than one percent of your audience will ever pick up the phone to call you, so be very careful in screening calls so that every one serves a point. Whether it is confrontation with the host, information, or entertainment, the caller should be used for a precise reason.

I also learned that you need to know your audience. Know who you're broadcasting to. If you're in Philly, you need to know that the Eagles are the most important thing in town. If you're in New York, it's the Yankees. Also at WIP, more than anywhere else, I also learned that you need an angle, and you need to live, breathe, and sleep the topics you're talking about with the same passion that your listeners do. Showing up and reading the newspaper was for lazy hosts with no ratings and no desire to be successful. I wanted to be a star, and I was willing to work harder than anybody else to become one.

Seven months after I got to WIP, I went to my first holiday party. I didn't bring a date, as I didn't know protocol. This turned out to be a good thing. After the cocktail hour, Bigby wanted to have all the on-air hosts come up onstage and say a word or two, and then conduct a raffle for the family members in attendance. One by one he called the various hosts until they were all up there, except for me and Jody McDonald, the midday host. I wasn't called up on the stage, not because I wasn't a valued member of the air staff, but because this was the type of mental game Bigby liked to play. He loved to make people feel uncomfortable, insecure, and inadequate.

Bigby had called Jody's name a few times, but he refused to go up. He refused because as he said, "If Craig isn't called up there, then I'm not going. He's as much a part of this staff as anyone." I never forgot that, and even though I still didn't get called up, I have always done everything I can for Jody over the years. I love him for what he did.

The second awkward moment at the party was with another station employee's wife. He and his wife had to be well into middle age, and while the staff member was sober that night because he had to drive home, his wife was liquored up. I was standing outside the bathrooms. She came up to use the facilities, only to find the women's room occupied. She struck up a conversation with me. Clearly intoxicated, she swayed back and forth. Then she let go the bombshell: "You're Craig, right?"

"Yes, I am," I said.

"Will you fuck me?"

"What . . . um, are you okay?"

"Will you fuck me? My husband can't get it up tonight and I need some cock. Will you fuck me in the bathroom? He'll never know. Please fuck me."

I told her I thought she'd had too much to drink, and that she should be careful what she was saying. "Then fuck you, if you can't give me any cock." She stumbled into the bathroom.

I didn't stay at the party much longer after that, but in retrospect, I guess I should have, just to see what else might have happened the more everybody drank.

One year later, I had established myself as one of the top reporters covering the Eagles. Norman Braman owned the team, and Eagles fans hated him. He wasn't a Philadelphian, didn't have the charisma to win anybody over, and had a general apathy for the city. I had gotten a phone call out of the blue from a trusted friend saying that Braman had agreed to sell the franchise to an unnamed person. "Fuck you," I said, but my friend reiterated that he had seen the deal and it would be announced soon. I could break the story right then and there.

Up to this point, the stories I had broken were your garden-variety: players being let go or acquired, who would start, and so on. This news was huge. I called Bigby up right away and told him what I had. He told me to talk to Angelo Cataldi off the air, because Cataldi had been a reporter for a long time, and he could help me vet the reporting. I called Cataldi. He didn't buy my info on face value. He told me I should call Harry Gamble, the Eagles' general manager, and see what he said.

I knew Gamble but didn't have a deep relationship with him at the time, as he was an older man on his last NFL legs. He didn't have time to get to know a young reporter. I called him anyway and got his secretary. I told her that I needed to speak with Gamble right away. She asked why, and I said it was urgent news and that I needed his time. She told me he wouldn't be free all day, and right there I had to make a decision whether to tell her why I needed to talk with Gamble *now*.

I said, "Ma'am, I am about to announce on WIP Radio that the Eagles have been sold. I can do that with or without talking to Harry. I'd like to be able to do it having talked with him." Dead silence for about ten seconds, then bam, Harry Gamble is on the phone. "Harry, it's Craig Carton. I am going to report that the Eagles have been sold. Do you have a comment for me?" "No comment," he said. And that was it. I had the goods, and now the Eagles knew it. I had to get on the air ASAP and report it before they did, or I would lose my scoop.

I called Cataldi off-air while he was hosting the morning show and told him what Harry said. He said that was enough for him to go with it. He put me on hold and said, "You're next." Sixty seconds later, as the morning show came out of a commercial break, I heard Cataldi say that WIP had a big announcement, and for the details here is Craig Carton.

I came on the air and said matter-of-factly that Norman Braman had sold the Eagles to a mystery buyer from the Northeast, and that the new owner would be in town that week. Pending formal NFL approval, the Eagles had been sold. Shazam! The biggest sports story to hit Philly since the death of Jerome Brown—and I had it before anyone else.

I called my contact and pleaded with him to tell me the buyer's name and background. After an hour of back-and-forth, I got it: Jeff Lurie was the new owner of the Eagles.

I called back in to the morning show and dropped the second bombshell. Lurie, who had no background in sports, was the NFL's newest owner. Jeff Lurie tells the story that he was sitting in the back of a cab in Philly on his way to the airport, convinced that there was no way anybody knew that he had just agreed to buy the Eagles. The cabbie had WIP on, and Lurie was listening at the moment I said his name. My report forced the Eagles and Jeffrey Lurie to hold a press conference earlier than they'd wanted to, to acknowledge that the story was accurate.

Breaking the story catapulted me to being a major presence on WIP, and as a reporter. Tom Bigby floated the idea of me moving from nights to middays to help the sagging ratings of the Jody McDonald and Glen Macnow show. Yet despite the success, I had no idea how I was perceived by the rest of the media in town. And I later found out that you never know who is listening at any given point in time, and how they will react to what you say—especially when you say it about them.

REVENGE OF THE PUSSY MAVEN 20

The ringing woke me up with the volume of a freight train. The phone must have rung no fewer than fifty times before I gave in, rolled over, and squinted at the time on the digital clock. It was 4:33 in the morning, and the phone wouldn't stop. I grabbed it and muttered, "Who the fuck is this?"

The voice on the other end came right to the point. "Yo, Craig, get your ass to room 810 right now."

"Huh, who is this?"

"It's *William Smithe*, muthafucka. Now get your ass to my room. We got a problem."

I had been out all night with William (not his real name) and seven other Eagles players. We were in Seattle on a Friday night in December 1995, a full two days before the Eagles were to play the Seahawks. The

Eagles were riding high, having won three straight games. They were expected to beat the Seahawks, who limped into the game with a 5–7 record.

Ray Rhodes, the head coach of the Eagles, knew better than to let a group of grown men worth millions of dollars hit the town for forty-eight hours before a game. Ray claimed at the time that he did it because he was concerned about traveling across country and then immediately playing a game. He figured—or so he said—that if he got there on Friday and gave the guys a chance to get acclimated, he'd have a better chance of winning.

The truth is that he'd promised the men a vacation day away from their families if they won the week before. So here I was at 4:33 in the morning, being ordered to go to room 810 in the Doubletree Hotel. Oh, I forgot to mention that there was usually an 11 p.m. curfew the night before the game, but since the game wasn't until Sunday, there was no curfew at all.

Genius.

The night itself was typical for this group of guys, me included: a big dinner with more drinks and shots than anyone should ever drink postcollege, and then right to the clubs. Everywhere we went, our group attracted the best-looking girls, and lots of them. I like to think it was because I was having a really good night, but when you travel with eight recognizable football players making millions, a leper with a rash could have a good night.

The evening ended about 3 a.m., after we closed down the top strip club in town. Even though the girls at every place were all over the group, we left together on the limo bus we had rented for the evening. No women joined us—on the bus, at least.

What the women—football groupies to their core—do is ingenious. They find out what hotel the team is at and try to get guys to give up their room keys. Without a key, you can't access the floor, since it's secured. Guys can't be seen bringing women up to their rooms, because it's a surefire way to get suspended or fined for breaking team rules, and it would fuck it up for everybody else. So they slip a girl the key at the club, tell them to head over, and by the time the player gets back, there's a naked woman waiting for him.

Or at least that's the plan. Apparently when the plan doesn't work, you call a hooker to come over instead, as I found out at about 4:37 that morning.

I threw a shirt on and stumbled down to room 810. I knocked and the door flew open. WS was expecting me. There were some players and their friends in the suite, and there was a lot of commotion and noise. I asked WS what was going on. "Look in there," he said, pointing to the bedroom. Before I even opened the door, I heard the problem. The problem was a shrieking twenty-something hooker with no top on and wearing what amounted to ripped spaghetti for underwear. She was pissed. I asked her what the problem was and she said, "Who the fuck are you?"

I turned to WS and said, "What's going on?" Before he could answer, the woman interrupted and said, "I'll tell you what the fuck is going on! These motherfuckers owe me money, and I ain't leaving till I get it."

"What do they owe you for?" I asked.

She snapped back at me, "I blew every one of these motherfuckers, and they got to pay me."

Before I could process that, she picked up the room phone and dialed 911. That call started the clock. Everyone would have to get to their rooms and pretend to be asleep before the police showed up.

I asked her what she was owed. To my astonishment, she replied one hundred dollars. A hundred bucks for blowing eleven guys, and these assholes wouldn't pay her? I turned to the group of men, each one big enough to squash me between his fingers, and said, "A hundred bucks, guys. Are you that stupid? Pay the woman!" And then I heard a line I will never forget:

"She wasn't any good. Fuck that bitch, I ain't paying her."

They were collectively worth north of $50 million, but they wouldn't give her $100. I grabbed WS, who had a new multiyear, multimillion-dollar deal, and said, "Scrape together three hundred dollars, or you are all fucked." After a lot of resistance, I had a pile of cash with singles, fives, and tens from the group. Cheap fucks, I thought. I gave the hooker the $300 and called hotel security. They escorted her out a back entrance, minutes before the police hit the floor. Thank God, nobody ever got caught.

Two days later, the Eagles lost by double digits to the Seahawks, and Ray Rhodes announced he would never fly to an away-game city on a Friday ever again.

After I broke the story about the Eagles being sold to Jeff Lurie, I was the new number-one source for Eagles news, and at the perfect time. Tom Sredenschek, the guy I hosted my first tryout show with, called me a few weeks later. He had become a well-respected sports producer and now was working on a new show on Spectacor that would be called *Eagles Magazine* or *Eagles Insider*. He and his team agreed that I would be a great host for the show, as I was now synonymous with the Eagles and would bring them some instant credibility and promotion through WIP.

I met with Tom and his group at Dirty Frank's, a downtown bar in Philly. It all went great. They laid out the show for me and their expectations, and we left with a handshake that we had a deal. The show would start two months from that meeting. Assuming we could agree on salary, we were as good as gold.

Tom Sredenschek called two days later. I assumed he was calling to make the official monetary offer. He was solemn, though, and began by saying he didn't know how to say it, but we had hit a snag. When he told the executives that I was going to be the host, there was a problem. It wasn't that I wasn't qualified or the right guy for the show. They agreed that I was. The problem was that Larry Rosen was an executive with Spectacor now, and was still the main host, too. He hadn't forgotten what I'd said about him on the Ugly Show. He agreed that I was the best man for the job, but insisted that we'd all have a face-to-face before he would green-light my being the host.

We all met the next day in the Spectacor offices and waited in a conference room until Larry came in. He was late on purpose, and came in with one thing in mind: making me pay for saying he was ugly. He walked into the room. I knew then that I had no shot at the job.

I also realized that I was right. He *was* the ugliest guy I had ever seen.

"So what's going on?" he asked with a wry smile. Tom explained that we were all set to go with the show, but we knew there was an issue with Larry and me, and we were hoping to work it out.

Larry looked right at me and said, "So am I the ugliest person you have ever seen on TV?"

"Larry, that show was more than a year ago. We were just having fun. You can't be mad about that still, are you?" I asked.

"Tell me to my face that I'm the ugliest guy you ever saw on TV." He wanted to embarrass and belittle me. So I went the other way. Knowing what he wanted, I refused to apologize. I said, "Larry, you gotta get over yourself and have a sense of humor." I took advantage of the undisputable truth that it's always good not to need a job when presented with another one. Had I been unemployed, the rest of the meeting might have been different. But as I was making more money than I ever thought I would, and I didn't need the TV job. I had control.

"Beg me for the job, Craig. Tell me how sorry you are for what you said, and beg me to let you work on my network."

"Not going to happen, Larry."

He went on a five-minute tirade about how much pussy he got and what a stud he was. He worked himself up with spit foaming at the corners of his mouth. I couldn't help but start laughing, which incensed him even more. "What the fuck is so funny? You don't think I get lots of pussy?"

"I don't know or care how much pussy you get; I just know that this is the single funniest thing I have ever seen, and you are still to this day the ugliest guy I've ever seen on television. But if you want the best show these guys can make, then I am the host. If not, so be it. I do have a day job. Thank you for your time." I walked out.

He chased me into the parking lot. "Carton!" he yelled. I turned around and he shouted, "I'm a pussy maven! I get more pussy than you could ever imagine! Pussy comes to me—I don't go after it!"

I didn't get the job.

The WIP midday show didn't do badly because it was a bad sports show. It did badly because it was a straight sports show, and because Glen Macnow was and is the single most boring radio person on the planet. If ever a guy must have had pictures of his boss, it was Macnow. He could fuck up a wet dream without even being in the same zip code.

Anyhow, I was becoming a bigger star there, and was making $100,000 when I resigned from my one-year deal. Bigby floated middays to me, and even represented it as guaranteed to happen, but he never came through with it.

At the same time that I had my first real fling with stardom, I acquired a legitimate stalker. Being single and having cash in my pocket, I went out just about every night of the week. When my shift ended at eleven or after a ball game, I went right out to Philadelphia's South Street, which had the hot bars all year long, or I went to Delaware Avenue outdoor bars in the summertime.

The summer of 1995 was no exception, and I got around. I was making up for not having any girls at the time of my bar mitzvah, and I made up for it every night that I could. Apparently there was a girl about my age who was a huge sports fan, who'd seen me from a distance and had begun telling her friends that we were dating.

I had no idea about this until one day I was at a bar and a woman came up to me and suddenly threw a drink on me. "You have some nerve doing what you did to Alyssa," she said.

"What are you talking about?" I asked.

She went on to say how rude it was of me to leave Alyssa at a bar earlier that evening, and then to start hitting on girls at this new bar. I had no idea what she was talking about, and after ten minutes, she figured out that I wasn't lying. She never apologized for the drink in my face but told me she knew where Alyssa was, and that for months she had been telling people we were dating.

Now, it was possible that I had forgotten a girl I hooked up with, but trust me, I wasn't dating anybody, and I wasn't in a relationship. I did, however, want to know what Alyssa looked like, and hoped that she was hot, if nothing else.

Later that night I was at Rock Lobster, an outdoor bar on the Delaware River, and I saw the group of girls who had accosted me earlier. One of my buddies said hi to them, and he was told that Alyssa was there. I spotted her from about twenty-five yards away, standing by herself, awkwardly looking in my direction but not knowing that I could see her. She was pretty but there was something wrong with her. Not something like she had a cleft palate or a limp, but something in-between-her-ears wrong with her. She had the runaway-bride look. I approached her and introduced myself, and asked her if she was all right. She muttered something, then turned and ran away.

I didn't think much of it until a few hours later. When my buddies and I got my back to our apartment, it was about four in the morning and we had a few girls with us. When we walked into the lobby, Alyssa was there waiting for me.

"Who is that you're with, and how dare you bring another woman home when you knew I would be waiting here for you?" she demanded.

Cuckoo for Cocoa Puffs. "Alyssa, you know we aren't dating. What are you talking about?" With that she went after the girl standing next to me. The front desk guy called the police, and we restored some order to the lobby. I told her that she had a choice: get arrested and have me press charges, or wake the fuck up and back off. She went home before the cops showed up, and I never thought another thing about her until the summer of 1997, two years later.

I had been approached by a guy named Ross Levinsohn who was running a company called CBS SportsLine down in Fort Lauderdale, Florida. He wanted to know if I had any interest in being nationally syndicated and moving to Florida. This same Ross Levinsohn years later would convince Rupert Murdoch to buy Myspace for $580 million, and years after that, would become interim CEO of Yahoo!

Levinsohn and I talked back and forth about it, and when the day came to make plans for me to come down and visit the company headquarters, he told me to call and set it up with the gal that answered the phone. I called, and a young woman said hello. I said, "My name is Craig Carton. Ross Levinsohn asked me to call to set up a trip down to see you guys."

Next I heard the following: "Uh, hi Craig, I've been waiting for your call. It's Alyssa. How have you been? I can't wait to start working with you!"

Unreal. It was my stalker, alive and well, about to become my co-worker.

DON'T BE THAT GUY 21

It may be my background, but I start puking whenever I show up for a company softball game and see a guy wearing full Major League Baseball attire. For some reason, it pisses me off.

I grew up playing ball in blue jeans and a T-shirt. Sadly though, there are men out there who think it is imperative to dress exactly like a professional. The only time it's ever appropriate for a nonprofessional athlete to dress like a pro is Halloween for the kids' sake, or when your name is Candy and you're about to dance to Def Leppard's "Pour Some Sugar on Me" for tips.

Actually, I've always been fascinated by the way women dress. Why, for example, do fat chicks wear spandex pants to the gym with the spandex Speedo shorts on top of the pants? It doesn't look good. It only accentuates their weight issues. Do they look in the mirror before they leave the house and say, "Oh yeah, I'm killing it today?" I also wonder when I go to a dance club and see hot and not-so-hot girls wearing miniskirts that wouldn't be long on a five-year-old. How do they think that guys don't assume they are easy and sex is guaranteed? Your vagina is on display every time you spin around. You had to know that when you left the house.

Even better, I have realized that women dress in packs, the way wolves hunt. So every girl that leaves the house to party has had her outfit analyzed and approved by a minimum of three other girls. "Oh yeah, sister, you look awesome; how do I look?" It's even funnier to me when the boyfriends of these tramps get pissed when other guys eye-fuck their women. It ain't our fault that your girl basically has a neon sign on that says, "I wanna have sex!" It's your fault for letting her out of the house like that.

But back to sportswear. Every time I see a guy with wristbands, stir-rups, and baseball pants getting ready to play in a Central Park softball league game, I want to punch him right in the face. It's softball! I show up barefoot in cargo pants and a tank top, hoping someone remembered to bring beer.

And it's not just softball games with these guys. It's the batting cages, their kids' Little League games, Wiffle ball outings. It's like they're desperate for attention, or desperate for someone to think because they dress like they can play, they must be able to play.

We've all seen these guys, and we all react the same way. At first we try to figure out who he is, then we watch him practice, and then we just laugh our asses off and mock him with our buddies. The best is when the guy has an actual player's name on the back of the jersey. Then we can refer to him by name: "Jeter's up . . . Wow, I can't believe Derek Jeter is playing softball with us . . . Hey, I struck out Derek Jeter in soft-ball . . . Wow, look at Jeter run . . . Hey Jeter, where's A-Rod?" and so on.

There's nothing worse than striking out in softball. I don't care if it's arc, modified, or fast-pitch, you've got to make contact. There's a difference between swinging for strike three and watching it fly right past you into the catcher's glove for the third strike. But either way, if you ever strike out in softball, it's time to retire your sneakers. If you lined a bunch of guys up in a police lineup, and you had a guy who peed his pants, a guy who was a premature ejaculator, a guy who likes to watch *Glee*, a guy in his thirties who still lives with his parents, a forty-year-old virgin, and a guy who struck out in softball—the guy who struck out would be the most embarrassing dude there.

I've tried a million times to understand these numbskulls who wear pro uniforms, and I just can't. Are they wearing the outfit to attract girls? Can't be, because there isn't a girl on the planet who would fall for a guy wearing eye black, stirrup socks, and a sweatband around his forearm, while lugging his gear in an Easton bat bag, along with whatever other stuff the pros seem to use. It can't be because he thinks that's the required outfit. Go to a softball game anywhere, and he'll be the only guy dressed that way.

So what is it that makes these douchebags think it's appropriate to dress up to play softball? And it isn't just softball. It's every sport.

I was once playing hoops at a sporting club in Cherry Hill, New Jersey, with some friends. A few other guys showed up and asked us to play full court. We were happy to oblige. One of them turned out to be a member of the group Boyz II Men (the tall one; not the chubby one, and not the really skinny one). When he took off his jacket and sweats, he was wearing an authentic Chicago Bulls Michael Jordan jersey and shorts. He had the socks and Air Jordans on, too. It was like he robbed the in-store mannequin that they dressed in Jordan's authentic gear to show you how cool MJ looked in it.

We couldn't stop laughing, but then we thought, There is no way some guy, and in this case he's a semi-famous guy, is going to go to a gym to run some ball and dress that way, unless he can play his ass off. Turns out, like most tools who dress up like professionals to play pickup sports, he couldn't play dead. He couldn't dribble, he shot the ball like he was from Mars, and he called a foul on every play. What a clown.

Some of you might be booshie and belong to a country club and have no idea what I mean, so next time you go to the club, spot the first guy dressed like Roger Federer with a tennis racket bag, tight white European shorts, and whatever else tennis players wear. It's the same exact guy we see playing softball dressed like Derek Jeter.

So we know it doesn't turn the ladies on, we know it doesn't indicate that they can play—what is it then? Well, I minored in psychology and learned all that Freud shit and Piaget garbage, and I've figured it out. After several shots of Reserva de la Familia tequila one night, the answer came to me. Why would any adult dress up like John McEnroe to play tennis, or like Albert Pujols to play softball, or like MJ to play hoops?

They're losers. End of story.

Don't be that guy. Nobody likes that guy; women won't fuck that guy; and nobody will give that guy a ride home after the game.

22 KARDASHIAN, WITHOUT THE ASS

The negotiations with Ross Levinsohn of SportsLine were taking forever. I insisted that he fly me into Fort Lauderdale, figuring I could close the deal face-to-face a lot quicker than on the phone. It was June 1997. I was fresh off a major scandal in Philadelphia regarding my report that Eric Lindros missed a game because he was hungover.

The story, which followed me my entire radio career, went like this:

On February 11, 1997, the Flyers played Ottawa and won the game; nothing newsworthy.

On February 13 and 15, they were set to have a home-and-home with the Pittsburgh Penguins.

Lindros missed the game on the 13th for what the team called "back issues," and then he missed the home game on the 15th, for the same reason. Problem was, they lied about why he missed the game on the 15th. As big as this story became, my "report" of it was as innocuous as possible and garnered no attention whatsoever for three full days.

Two weeks later, on February 28, I was filling in for Steve Fredericks and cohosting the afternoon show on WIP with Mike Missanelli. We were live from a Slack's Hoagie Shack in New Jersey.

At one point during the show, the Flyers were being discussed, and a caller phoned in to say how upset he was. He could only afford to take his kid to one game a year, and he chose February 15. They felt let down that Lindros wasn't on the ice. Lindros was his son's favorite player. I commented, "And it's a real shame that he missed the game because he was hungover." We said goodbye to the caller, and then Mike asked me what I meant. "He missed the game because he was hungover from Valentine's Day celebrating, and frankly if I were him, I would be doing the same thing, but I would have made it in to work the next day," I said. End of conversation.

For the next two hours of the show, we did not take a single call about it. We never brought it up again. It was a nonissue. Saturday, nothing said or written about it anywhere.

Sunday, not a single article or column or call to the radio station. I hadn't even thought about it again.

Monday morning, Mr. Boring, Glen Macnow, joined Angelo Cataldi and Al Morganti on the WIP morning show. Macnow brought up the story to Morganti, saying how irresponsible I was on Friday. The three of them proceeded to do a whole segment on it without ever calling me or checking to see why I said what I said. Two hours later, Eric Lindros missing the game was the single biggest sports story in America. I was smack-dab in the middle of it.

I was an established reporter by then, and I felt that I had the story buttoned down from multiple sources. I had also spent a good portion of Valentine's Day evening within twenty feet of Lindros, so I knew firsthand how much he was drinking.

My phone starting blowing up from reporters and TV stations and magazines around the country, and then Bigby called and demanded that I come in to the station to talk.

"Nothing to talk about, Tom."

"Get your ass in here now."

My meeting with Tom was frustrating. He kept demanding to know my sources, which I refused to give up. He wanted to know because the station was in the middle of negotiating a new deal to carry Flyers games. I was sure that he was going to turn my sources over to the team, and I was not going to let that happen.

I never claimed I was Woodward or Bernstein, but I would never dick over a source, either, so Tom and I went round and round for an hour. At no point did I ever reveal to him the numerous sources I had.

I couldn't figure out why this became such a big story, but it did. I was the front-page story of *Hockey News,* and I was the entire back-page column of *Sports Illustrated.* Front page on both Philly newspapers. Every major news organization was waiting outside my apartment so they could get a comment. I was Kim Kardashian, but without the hot sisters, and not nearly as nice an ass. I decided to allow Vai Sikahema to come into my building with a cameraman and hang with me in my apartment. Vai, a former Eagle, was the main sports anchor for the NBC affiliate in Philly, Channel 10. He had become a close friend, and I figured that while I wouldn't talk on camera, the least I could do for a friend was allow him access to me and let his cameraman take some video of the two of us talking on my couch.

This type of TMZ drama went on for days and weeks as the team announced that it was going to sue the radio station and me. The station covered me for any costs involved, but this meant that I would have to talk with lawyers every day for nearly a month. I told anyone who would listen to ask the Flyers why he missed the games, and what he was doing during them. The first excuse they had was that Eric had been hit hard in the game against Ottawa and couldn't play at his expected level. Regarding his whereabouts on February 14, they first claimed that he was home alone watching movies he had rented from Blockbuster.

I went on the air that night and said that would be easy to prove, and if they could prove it, then I would admit that I was wrong and take any punishment from the station. They never produced the proof. The next night they claimed that he was in a hyperbaric chamber all of the evening of the 14th, and couldn't have been out drinking. I asked where the hyperbaric chamber was, and how he came to use it, but they never produced any evidence of him being in one.

Ed Snider, the owner of the team, came after me. He hired one of the most prominent attorneys in Philly to sue me. The Flyers saw this dustup as an opportunity to fight back against a station that had been critical of them over the years for their lack of playoff success. My story, if that's what you want to call it, came on the heels of a story Mike Missanelli reported that Eric had given his personal Flyers tickets to Joey Merlino, the acting underboss of the Philadelphia mob. That story sent the Flyers through the roof, and they denied it until a picture of Merlino sitting in Eric's seats popped up in the *Philadelphia Daily News*. (Lindros never denied giving him his tickets.) The Flyers were looking for something, anything, to attack the credibility and success of the radio station. I was their man.

The Lindros family was incensed, as well. As overprotective parents, they ran the Flyers in those days, and Bonnie Lindros, Eric's overbearing mother, who once cost Eric the Campbell's Soup deal and a guaranteed Flyers contract of nearly $75 million, went ballistic. She knew the story was accurate, and interestingly enough, she wasn't mad at me. She went after the Flyers because she wanted to know who told me the story. The Lindros family, Eric included, have never once said a bad word about me, but they unleashed a holy war inside the walls of the Spectrum, where the Flyers played.

Bonnie had executives checking phone records to try to figure out who the snitch was. Sadly, they all settled on a young woman I had known for a few years. She and I would chat from time to time. Phone records showed that we talked the week of the report. That's all they needed to pounce. They had their Deep Throat.

The public rhetoric went on for weeks, as did the on-air banter, until the lawyers representing me told me that with WIP and me in the middle of litigation with the Flyers, I shouldn't talk about it in public.

Fellow hosts went after me like I was a demon. They were relentless. I never revealed my sources. I never once played the voice mails left for me from prominent players saying how sorry they were that they couldn't back me up. I never told half of what I knew.

I kept my mouth shut, as directed by my attorneys. The station ultimately came to an agreement with the Flyers and came up with the following: The station would say that the story was false, but say that I still thought it to be true, which I did, and thus there was no actual slander of Eric or the team. In return, they would make a donation to Eric's charity, and the case would be closed.

I was incensed that I couldn't speak about the story publicly but grateful to CBS for having my back through the entire ordeal. Not only did they defend me but they also never threatened me with being fired and could not have been more supportive.

I had been punked.

•   •   •

For the next five years, no matter where I went and no matter who showed an interest in hiring me, someone asked about the Lindros case. Three years later, I was doing mornings in New York City at WNEW Radio and got wind of a newspaper report in which Bobby Clarke said, and I quote: "The kid from WIP was right; Eric was drunk."

Ed Snider even got into the act at a press conference when the relationship between Eric and the team had soured. He hinted that reporters should follow up on the story, and another story about Eric that had never been published in which he almost bled to death after being in a single-car accident.

My story first broke in February 1997. I left WIP in the late summer of that year. The case wrapped up in the spring of 1998. I was never fired, and I was never punished for the story, but there are people who would swear that both happened.

When Bigby didn't live up to his pledge to make me the new midday guy, I wanted out. I was miserable doing nights and Eagles. Ross Levinsohn provided me the opportunity to leave. Since negotiations were dragging on the phone, I told Ross that my sister had just been accepted to a college in Florida and that I would be in town for twenty-four hours to help her move into her dorm. As long as I was there, I might as well come in to the office and knock the deal out face-to-face.

Ross and I had only met once, and that was at the CBS March Madness kickoff party. That's when he first asked me if I wanted to work for SportsLine. It had been about four months, and I was trying to set myself up for the next chapter of my life. He agreed that seeing each other in person was a great idea. I flew down first thing in the morning, rented a car, and drove to the Fort Lauderdale office of SportsLine.

I walked in, and the first person I saw was Alyssa, my Philly stalker. She was pleasant, and told me how excited she was that she'd be working alongside me. She was producing an Internet-only radio show hosted by Scott Kaplan and Sid Rosenberg. They had been doing this show that nobody could hear for about six months.

I was brought into Ross's office, and he jumped up from his desk, gave me a huge hug, and said, "Welcome, let's get a deal done." The deal was complicated. They didn't have tons of cash, because they were not yet public, but they did have a shitload of stock options.

Ross offered me $65,000, all moving expenses, the first two months' rent, and 30,000 options of stock with the purchase price of $4. I would also be allowed to invest another 50 percent of my yearly salary into the stock, and I was allowed a onetime purchase equal to another 50 percent of my yearly salary. All in all, I was looking at 70,000 options of SportsLine stock at a purchase price of $4. I would be vested in one year. There was no state income tax in Florida, I was young and single, and I figured that to get out of Philly and move to South Florida was worth a few less bucks when the potential windfall could be huge. We were right in the middle of the dot-com stock boom, and guys all over the world were becoming instant millionaires. The other great aspect of the deal was that Ross guaranteed me instant syndication on a minimum of forty stations. We shook hands and I agreed to the deal. I flew back to Philly the same day and prepared to give WIP notice that I was leaving.

Bigby was great, and wished me well, as did only one host on the radio station. They were still all so full of themselves months after the Lindros nonsense that none of them had the class to say good luck or goodbye except for Howard Eskin. I never forgot Eskin's gesture, and never will.

When I had gotten to Philly in 1993, I was raw. I was leaving as a seasoned reporter and talk show host who knew what he wanted and how to deliver a great show daily. Being on the air at WIP Radio from 1993 to 1997 made me. The next three jobs I got were a direct result of my working at WIP, because every programmer in the country wanted to replicate the WIP success. I wound up hating Tom Bigby, but I never would have gotten good at radio if I hadn't worked for him. I still hate him and respect him just as much today as I did when I left WIP.

During my four-plus years in Philly, I also opened and operated a successful tavern known as Labradors Pub, which has enough stories for a whole other book. There I met the love of my life and future wife, Kim—but more on that in a later chapter.

I arrived in Florida on Labor Day weekend of 1997. The first order of business was to find a place to live, and the second was to decide if I would do a solo show, or bring in a partner. I had decided to bring my own producer with me from WIP. His name was Bill Matoney, and he was already on his way down to Florida.

Bill wasn't a real producer. He was a kid who ran the board at WIP. All that meant was that Bill was in charge of pushing a button with any finger he chose to start the automated commercial break. He also had to answer the phone when people called in to be on the air with me. We got along, and he would do anything for me. I thought it was important to have someone I knew I could trust 100 percent watching my back. I didn't know anything about the people who worked at SportsLine, other than the girl who'd stalked me. Matoney was an insurance policy. Hiring him proved to be shrewd a year later.

Sixty-five grand ain't a shitload to live off, and you can't buy a huge house, but I found a two-bedroom bottom-floor town house with amazing pools, a rec center, basketball courts, and every other amenity you would want a development to have, for seven hundred dollars a month.

●　　●　　●

My first day of work, I had a powwow with Ross about the show. He was clear that I was in charge of all show decisions, but he wanted me to consider a woman as a cohost. Apparently this woman was desperate to be on the air, had done some reporting and freelance work here and there, and was working for the company already. Ross asked me to take her out to lunch to see if our personalities could mesh, and added that he would be thankful if I could make it work with her.

I soon learned this woman had little to no radio experience, and yet had an inexplicable sense of entitlement. She had never been on the radio in any real capacity and yet felt that she should not only have a show, but also be syndicated right away. Her one claim to fame was that her parents were well-known Hollywood writers who cowrote several episodes of a popular TV show. She'd had a bit role in one episode.

We met at a restaurant for the first time, and I was amazed that she started right in about what type of show we were going to host and how she had all these plans. I engaged her for about twenty minutes, which was nineteen minutes more than I could take, until I'd had enough. The hot waitress came over three times, but she sent her away and told her that we weren't ready to order yet. I like a strong, take-charge gal, but I was ready for some artichoke and spinach dip, a stiff drink, and the waitress's phone number.

Finally I stopped her and said matter-of-factly, "Do you know why we are having lunch today?" She replied, "Yeah, to talk about our show." I started to laugh and told her there was no show just yet. We were having lunch because Ross wanted to see if I liked her and if we could get along. Her entire demeanor changed. She pouted for the rest of the meal. I told her that whomever I worked with would be in a secondary role and have to play off me, and be comfortable with that. She wasn't happy, and strangely enough, that made me happy.

After lunch, and my not getting the waitress's phone number, I had to meet with Ross again to let him know what I thought of her as a potential cohost. I told him I thought she was high-maintenance, and would struggle in any role in radio. He responded with one of the greatest lines ever for a guy who wanted to make sure someone got hired: "I'll give you five thousand more shares of stock if you give her a shot." Bang, just like that we had a show that CBS SportsLine decided to call *Sports Uncensored.*

The only way I could get anything out of my new cohost was to empower her, and I did that by making her into what turned out to be a Robin Quivers type of character. In the last hour of our four-hour show, we would go over the biggest sports stories of the day on a national level. I gave her the task of independently preparing the stories, and sound bites, and delivering them to me on-air without any oversight.

For the other three hours, she would be a bit player and comment on or react to what I was doing in limited doses. I think she was just happy to have the job. She actually took to the role well. She and I were getting along, the show was good—not great, but coming along—and everyone seemed happy. We were syndicated through Sports Fan Radio on forty-four stations throughout the country.

As my cohost and I concentrated on our radio product, Ross couldn't focus anymore because the company was getting ready to go public. The radio part of it was small potatoes compared to the overall picture. The only reason they got into radio was that their CEO wanted people to hear his product, SportsLine, and not have to have Internet to see it as they barnstormed around the country looking for investors and investment houses to back the IPO. As such, I saw Ross less and less. He then made a decision that changed the course of my career and life, for the worse.

He hired a program director to run the radio department so that he could concentrate on the rest of the company. The guy he hired was Charlie Barker. To me, Charlie seemed like a sloppy radio hack with limited experience as a director. Charlie was well into his thirties. He had most likely never seen a vagina up close.

My first introduction to Charlie was via a revealing conference call. During the call, Scott Kaplan, who, as I said, did a show with Sid Rosenberg, and who had as much radio experience as a leaky hose, tried to act as though he were Charlie's point person at SportsLine and control the call. I had more experience than the entire radio department combined, but a conference call with complete strangers wasn't where I was going to flex my muscle. I patiently listened to what Charlie had to say about his philosophy and what the future would hold. Charlie was going to start at the Super Bowl in 2008, and that would be our first chance to meet him. How exciting.

At the time, things with me and my partner were fine, although she spent as much time creating a mural on the wall by her desk as she did preparing for the show. I asked her what the mural was all about, and she replied that it was her wish list. Her wish list for what? She said matter-of-factly, "My wish list of guys I want to meet before I die." The mural consisted of photos of every African-American actor who had ever had a starring role in a movie, and African-American all-stars in every sport. Always good to have goals, I thought. You go, girl!

We were going to San Diego along with Scott and Sid. My cohost flew out separately to see her folks first. Scott and Sid both thought their shit didn't stink and that they had the greatest show in the world, although neither had ever done radio at any level prior to this. Sid had been doing customer service at SportsLine while hiding from numerous gambling debts he had back in New York. I found Sid engaging. I thought Scott was pompous.

We landed in San Diego, and Sid and I shared a cab to the hotel. He told the driver that we needed to make a stop on the way. "A stop for what?" I wanted to know. Sid said he had to pick something up, and told the driver to take him to the worst neighborhood in San Diego. He needed to find some crack. He handed the driver a twenty-dollar bill.

Time-out. I'm not going, so you can either let me out here, or you can visit the crack den after I go to the hotel. Sid agreed, dropped me off, and then went on his way. I had seen cocaine in large quantities at college, and had smoked pot, tried 'shrooms and ecstasy. But crack—come on, dude, really!

We all had to make a public appearance at a happy hour bar in San Diego. We agreed to meet at Scott and Sid's room twenty minutes before we had to be at the bar. My cohost was coming in to town later, and after the appearance we were supposed to have dinner and meet our new boss, Charlie Barker.

I went to their room and knocked on the door. A friend of Sid's opened it, and what I saw next stunned me. I walked into the room, and there was a smoking and dirty crack pipe, just like you'd see in the movies or on TV. Sid's friend had about fifteen joints rolled up and on display on the table.

Who the fuck smokes crack, and who needs fifteen joints at one time? I wondered. Sid's buddy offered me a joint. I said no. Not because I didn't get high at the time, but because I had a rule that I would never do it in front of people I didn't know well. Getting high might not be that big a deal, but I never wanted a stranger to be able to tell people that they saw me doing it.

Sid didn't offer me any crack.

I told the guys I would meet them in the lobby and walked out. The appearance went well. I was particularly amazed at Sid's ability to carry on conversation. I had a preconceived notion that a guy who smokes crack couldn't do that, yet he carried on with ease. Impressive, I thought.

After the appearance we met Charlie, a nebbishy, poorly dressed guy who looked like he came out of a Garanimals shopping disaster. This was our new boss. We were all there except for my cohost, and that was the beginning of the end for me. I was supposed to call her and let her know where dinner was, and she was going to meet us there. Well, I forgot to call her, and she didn't have anybody's number or a way to get a hold of anybody, so she sat in her hotel room steaming mad that we had the dinner without her, and she blamed me for it. I think she believed I was trying to get rid of her.

She was wrong, of course, but it didn't matter. When I saw her later that night at the hotel, she let me have it. She told me that she wasn't going anywhere, no matter how hard I tried to ditch her. This job meant everything to her. It gave her a platform to prove that women could do sports talk, something important to her. I told her she was nuts. She went ballistic again and said that she would get me before I got her.

I didn't think much of it at the time, but I should have.

For the next few weeks and months, she was cold to me, and working together became strained, all because of one missed dinner. Nothing else changed until midsummer. I had decided to placate Charlie with his need to have postshow meetings, but at the end of the day, I did the show the way I wanted. We had grown to about fifty-three affiliates.

I knew she was having a lot of meetings with Charlie without me, and she and I went a good three months without talking before our show, which was hard to do, considering we shared an office.

The company went public in the summer of 2008 and was a huge success. The stock price climbed through the teens and into the 20s, and then even higher. Each dollar the stock price rose meant $50,000 to me. I was less than two months away from vesting a portion of the stock that would have given me the right to sell about 20,000 shares. When the stock hit $30, I would have $600,000 banked. Like most people in the company, I was waiting to sell to guarantee the cash.

If I was there for a full year to the day and sold my available stock at the average price, I would have pocketed $700,000. If I had sold at its peak, I would have made $1.6 million; and had I been there for two years, I would have made more than $2 million at its average price, and more than $5.5 million at its peak. I had a one-year deal by design with an option for another year.

About six weeks before my one year was up and my option kicked in, we had on a basketball player name Michael Stewart from the Sacramento Kings. The Kings were terrible, and it interested me that Michael Stewart had been an all-American at high school and a stud in college, yet had probably lost more games this one year in the NBA than he had his entire life. "What's it like to play for a team that sucks?" I asked him.

That one question would change the course of my career. He answered the question, we finished the interview, and nothing came of it. It was an innocuous question.

After the show, Barker came to set up his daily postshow meeting and said to me, "Great show today! I loved it. Especially the interview with the player."

Now, at this point, my relationship with Barker wasn't great. He knew that there was nothing he was going to teach me or tell me to make me better. He knew I had worked for Bigby and been a Top 5–Arbitron rated host in three different major radio markets, and that Ross hired me directly. We were cordial, but that was it.

Right after the compliment, my partner chimed in. With a disgusted look, she said that she thought the question was insulting and embarrassing, and that we put the company in a bad light with the NBA.

I laughed. "In what way did we embarrass him or put the NBA in a bad light?" I asked.

"How dare you ask him what it's like to play for a team that sucks?" she said. "That's insulting to the Kings organization."

The Kings were 27–55 that year, and a laughingstock in the NBA. Trust me, I didn't embarrass anyone.

You could see a light—albeit a dim one—light up in Charlie's head. He suddenly agreed with her. This was their chance to get me by claiming that I had disrespected the entire NBA by saying the Kings sucked. SportsLine would have to do something about it.

I looked them both in the face and told them that if Stewart were on again, I would do it again; and if another player from a lousy team was on, I would ask them the question as well.

The name of the show, after all, was *Sports Uncensored*. I reminded Charlie that thirty seconds ago, he'd told me the show and the interview were great. "Well, now that I see it through what your partner said, I take it back; she's right," he said.

"You 'take it back'? What are we, nine-year-olds?"

Charlie stormed out of the room, and I left for home.

The next day, my cohost had a smirk on her face all morning. Again we did not speak before the show. Afterward, I was messing around on the computer when Charlie came into the office and asked if he could have a word with me. I said sure, and I followed him not toward his office, but toward Ross's. When I walked in, the head of Human Resources was there and Ross was behind his desk. Ross could not make eye contact with me and kept his head down the whole time. What a pussy.

Charlie said that due to my telling him that if the opportunity arose again, I would ask a player the same question, I had overstepped my bounds. I was being fired.

I looked right at Ross and said, "Ross, you're going to let him fire me for no reason and just sit there and do nothing about it?" Ross muttered something under his breath, like "I hired Charlie to run the radio division, so I have to let him run it."

I looked over at the HR director, who was also a friend and was on my softball team outside of work. He said, "Craig, I have some papers for you to fill out regarding the stock."

"Papers for what?"

"Well, since we are firing you for cause, you will forfeit all of your stock options."

There it was! It wasn't enough to fire me for some bullshit reason. They wanted to bury me. I told them they could all fuck off.

As I walked out the door, Ross never looked up from his desk. To make matters worse, the HR director, at whose house I had been drinking until four in the morning the weekend before, followed me to my office, watched me pack up my desk, and escorted me out of the building.

I was unemployed for the first time in my life. I seriously considered suing the company but decided to engage them personally instead, and after three years of lengthy discussions we privately agreed on a settlement. I felt vindicated, but by then I had worked for two radio stations in Denver, had been number one at both, and was now doing mornings at the legendary WNEW in New York.

THE GOOD STUFF 23

I met my wife, Kim, back in 1996 at Labradors Pub in Philadelphia. I owned and operated Labradors with three friends as an $80,000 investment that we all shared. We named it Labradors because we had two black Labs named Mason and Jordan, named after Anthony Mason and Michael Jordan. We had a huge wall that our patrons adorned with pictures of their Labs and other dogs. We opened on November 2, 1995, and were the single hottest bar in all of Philly for nearly two years. We made good money, but not great. We treated the bar as our own personal match.com, and there I had two of the most memorable social years of my life. And then one day Kim came in with her best friend. Her friend was a huge sports fan and had a crush on me, having become a devout listener of my radio show on WIP.

She heard that I had opened a bar, and asked Kim to be her wing

woman one night because she wanted to see me. When they walked into the bar, I was knocked off my feet by Kim. Her friend had no shot from that moment on. Kim acted forward in getting me to go out with her friend. I kept turning the conversation back to her, but she chewed on a straw while telling me she had a boyfriend. She did have a boyfriend, but I didn't care, I was hooked.

I got the girls their drinks, and Kim was having vodka and grapefruit juice. Our juice came out of the soda gun. It wasn't fresh by any stretch. When she complained about the taste, I told her that if she ever came back in, with or without her friend, I would have fresh grapefruit for her and personally squeeze it into her drink.

After that night, we started to talk frequently on the phone, but since this was before I had a cell phone, I either had to call her from home or, to avoid her boyfriend knowing it was me, I would call from random pay phones throughout Philly. After months of going on day dates like Rollerblading, it was clear that she made me feel different than I'd ever felt before. Not only was she beautiful with a great personality, but she played hard-to-get. The combination was irresistible. Sadly, though, she had a boyfriend, and I wound up moving to Florida before I ever found out if we worked as a couple. We didn't talk for six months after I moved, but I thought about her all the time. I hadn't ever done that with any other girl. I'd never had a girlfriend. I'd only had tons of one-night relationships. These new feelings were weird to me, but so real that I could not ignore them.

On my birthday, January 31, 1998, I got an anonymous gift in the mail; a cool candle, a candle holder, and balloons. I tracked down where they came from and called the store in Philly that sent them. The owner told me he had strict orders from the customer not to say anything about who she was. I said, I just have one question then: was she wearing Rollerblades? He said yes, and I knew they were from

Kim. She basically lived in her blades. I lit the candles that night, so that she could be in my house with me on my birthday. Unfortunately, I put the candles too close to my ceiling, and while I wasn't paying attention, they ignited the paint. I had a full-fledged fire in my house. I laughed and figured it was meant to be.

Shortly after that, I got word through one of her friends that she was coming down to South Beach for a wedding and wanted to get together. We met at an outdoor bar with all of her girlfriends and a few of my buddies. I was nervous walking into the bar, and when I saw her, I felt something that only she made me feel. I think you call it love—or lust—I don't know for sure, but I felt it. We spent the next night together, and I did the dumbest thing ever. She told me she would sleep over so we could maximize our time together while she was in town, and I felt that I had to take control of the relationship. Since she had a boyfriend and thus had control of our budding romance, I figured I needed to let her know that I now held the reins. I told her I didn't want her to stay over, and drove her back to her friend's house. She was pissed. She not only refused to see me the next day, she moved her flight up. We didn't talk again for almost a year, and I felt like an asshole to have let her get away.

A year later I was in Denver, Colorado, bored and alone on Christmas Eve, when I decided to call her out of the blue. She called me right back. We talked all night, and she agreed to fly out to Denver to see me. I had a better idea. My friend Marc Lawrence and I had started a company called Vegas Experts, and he called me to tell me a huge advertiser wanted to guarantee us $1 million, and we needed to meet with them in New York City. I told Kim to meet me at the airport in New York, and that we could go out in the city.

She picked me up as planned, and again I had that feeling. It was awesome. We went out that night with my friends, and I told her that while I was in my meeting the next day, she could hang out with my pals and that we would then go out alone at night. What I didn't know was that there was no meeting. My parents had conspired with Marc Lawrence to throw me a surprise thirtieth birthday party. Kim would now meet every living relative I had all at once, and she had brought nothing appropriate to wear. The party went great, though. Kim can talk to anybody from any background as easily as I talk on the radio. It's a great gift she has.

The weekend went so well that she agreed to fly out to Denver for Valentine's Day. Before she left, I asked her to move out there with me. She agreed, and she moved to Denver for good on April 1. We were engaged three months later, married three months after that, and she was pregnant three months after that. It was a great love story. Kim was my first and only true love, and as corny and clichéd as that concept is, it's the truth.

For the good adult stuff, the career success and the personal victories, I can only take some of the credit, as the majority of it goes to two other people: my ridiculously devoted and awesome wife, Kim, and my personal saint. He will remain unnamed because that's how he'd like it to be. These are the only two people in the world whom I have ever let inside the wall that I keep up, and who know the real, unedited me.

I never would have gotten to New York as a radio talent if not for my wife, even though it was a stroke of luck that I did. I never would have had the rare opportunity to return, if not for the advice and friendship of my saint.

I am forever grateful because without them, I'd be waiting tables somewhere, living alone and not experiencing the joy that life can bring. I would also have more kids than Antonio Cromartie—and God only knows how many baby mamas.

THE GREATEST TRADE OF ALL 24

We often talk about the great trades in sports, but the single greatest trade for me took place back in 1985. I was a camp counselor, and I fancied the lifeguard. She was friends with another counselor. He claimed dibs on her. As any man knows, dibs is an acceptable thing among friends. Rules of dibs: you can't dib a girl just because you saw her first, and you can't dib a girl just because she's hot and you want to bang her. You can, however, dib a girl that you have put time into, and a girl that you met first and want to ask out.

Dibs does come with a statute of limitations. If you met a girl and called dibs, but then never called her or went out on a date with her, dibs are over after a couple of weeks. Similarly, if the girl doesn't show an interest in you, you must undib her and give your crew a shot, and you have to put in a good word for whoever is next in line.

So here I was in 1985. This lifeguard had a smoking body. I had also just met Eric, who was a tennis counselor at the camp, and he said he knew her and was pursuing her. After two weeks of him getting nowhere, I told him it was time to undib her and man up. He agreed, with an interesting caveat. We had only been friends for a few weeks, so we didn't know each other that well, but he had gone out drinking with me and my friends one night when my younger sister tagged along. My sister is attractive. She looks like me with boobs. She's hot, and she liked to party and have a good time. Eric was smitten with her, as many men have been.

He proposed the following: Not only would he undib the lifeguard, but he would go out of his way to talk me up and set the path for a free and easy hookup. Then, in return, I would do the same for him with my sister.

Done deal.

I knew my sister wouldn't like him, because he was preppy, and she liked guys to be more of a challenge. So on that summer day in 1985, I traded my sister for the lifeguard. This is the same girl I wrote about earlier, the one I dry-humped for an hour because I couldn't get below her belt.

Anyway, as great as this trade was, it wasn't close to the trade between Yankee pitchers who traded wives one off-season. *Wives,* mind you.

Fritz Peterson and Yankee teammate Mike Kekich swapped wives back in 1972. Now, we have all heard of guys swapping uniform numbers and even cars from time to time, but these two consummated the single craziest trade in the history of Major League Baseball—and that includes the Red Sox giving Babe Ruth to the Yankees.

The guys and their wives were close, as many teammates and their families are. They spent a considerable amount of time together in the off-season. Peterson and Kekich were even closer than most. They had been best friends since 1969. They were both married at about the same time, had kids the same ages, and lived in New Jersey near each other.

The swap happened in 1972, but since the world lacked TMZ or Deadspin, they kept it quiet until the spring of 1973. The announcement led New York Yankees general manager Lee MacPhail to say, "We may have to call off Family Day." Fritz came on my radio show in 2011 and said that the real story was that they traded families, not just spouses. Each man just moved into the other guy's house and inherited the kids, the dogs, the mortgage payments, and, yes, the bedroom, along with the other man's wife.

Fritz got the better of the trade, as he is still married to Kekich's former wife, and had four children with her. Mike Kekich and Marilyn Peterson divorced soon after. Peterson's pitching suffered in 1973 after this "deal," and he was booed in nearly every ballpark. In April 1974, the Yankees traded him to the Indians.

Kekich never won more games than he did in 1972, the year he won ten.

EVERY VAGINA IN THE FREE WORLD

When I was growing up, the day the *Sports Illustrated* swimsuit edition hit the newsstands was the biggest day of the year. It ranked right up there with my birthday, Halloween (when I was allowed to trick-or-treat), and the Major League Baseball All-Star Game.

Decades before the Internet and sites like redtube.com, the swimsuit edition was a noncreepy way to ogle hot girls. The only other way at the time was to hope that your father had some *Playboy*s hidden under his mattress, or that you had an older brother who could score one for you.

My father had a loaded gun under his mattress, but no porn. There are days I think that I might have been conceived in an immaculate manner. Now, I'm not saying I'm the son of God or anything; I'm just saying my parents seemed to be antiromantic. And that's probably a good thing. Who wants to see their folks getting it on?

I have always felt that the *SI* swimsuit edition was more erotic than *Playboy*. You could close your eyes and imagine a hot girl in a bikini coming out of the ocean and interacting with you to the point of getting it on. With *Playboy*, there was nothing left to the imagination, and as a kid of the 1970s and early '80s, I'd say the women had a grooming problem, too. There was this one girl though, a Spanish vixen named Velasquez whom I had a major crush on. There was nary a day when I was thirteen that she and I didn't have a romantic private moment.

As time went on, the swimsuit edition became less relevant. There was the monthly Frederick's of Hollywood catalog that featured a hot blonde with see-through nipple tops; then Victoria's Secret started mailing out catalogs, and everything changed. Long gone were the days when Kathy Ireland in a one-piece suit was enough to get a young boy through the night after his parents told him to turn off the radio and go to bed.

Also long gone were big-boned girls wearing bloomers. In were thin, almost anorexic big-chested girls of the type you just don't see walking the streets that much. I'd like to know where they find these girls. I don't think I have ever seen a "model" that wasn't a real model, and I live in New York City, where there are more pretty women per square foot than any other city in the world. Yet I never see this model type anywhere. There must be some European or Brazilian factory where these women are made.

But then something went terribly wrong. In a move of desperation, *SI* started putting athletes and their attractive wives in the edition. At that moment they jumped the shark, and I stopped buying it until Irina Shayk graced the cover in 2011.

Isn't it enough that the athletes are good-looking and loaded? Now we have to have their hot wives thrown in our faces, too.

If you are a wealthy professional athlete, why get married at all? Derek Jeter should be the model for all pro athletes. He dated actress Minka Kelly for a long time. You never saw Derek get married or profess his undying love for a woman, ever. When word spread that Minka was spending some extra time with a movie costar, Jeter did the Jeterian thing. He moved on, and began dating a twenty-two-year-old Ralph Lauren model. All single men should live their lives by the WWDJD code: What Would Derek Jeter Do?

Better than that was the story from 2008 when not one or two, but three girls claimed to have spent the night with Jeter at a hotel in Florida. All three complained that after kicking them out, Jeter wouldn't validate their parking. That's right, you don't validate parking. You're Derek Jeter. They are lucky to have been with you. They can pay for their own fucking parking! And even now, you don't see him getting married.

A-Rod learned the lesson a little late, but he learned it. He was married to an attractive gal named Cynthia, had a few kids with her, and then got caught with blond strippers in Canada. Why'd he get married in the first place? Most people lashed out against him for the infidelity, but not me. I was upset that he got married. When you're a rock star like A-Rod, how dare you not enjoy the many options out there? I would be disappointed if guys like A-Rod didn't take advantage of who they were and conquer as many broads as possible.

Tiger Woods fell victim. Now, Tiger is a special case. Perhaps the most vilified guy of the last decade, and for what? Ooh, he cheated on his wife. How dare he? Tiger proves my point better than anyone, and here's why. His ex-wife Elin is a beautiful blond model. There isn't a guy on the planet who wouldn't want her to be on his arm, or to have the chance to sleep with her. And yet here is Tiger not just cheating on her, but cheating on her with every vagina in the free world. He either got bored banging her, or he realized how many girls would sleep with him, no matter what state or country he was in. I imagine he figured, *This is my birthright; if I don't do this, I'm an idiot and letting mankind down.*

It may be hard to understand, but somewhere in the world, there is a guy tired of banging the woman he is with, no matter how hot she is. Case in point: Halle Berry has been through how many husbands? And she might be the hottest woman of all time. Jennifer Aniston can't keep a man, Kate Moss can't keep a man, Bar Refaeli can't hang on to Leonardo DiCaprio . . . All stunning women, and all of them unable to keep a man. Maybe they have a fatal flaw. Maybe they are lousy in bed. Or maybe it goes back to the fact that any guy who can land a girl like them can also land other girls like them, so they do. Then there is Eva Longoria, another hot actress. She married Tony Parker of the NBA, and he did what I expected of him. He was hitting on girls at his own wedding. She then moved on to Jets starting QB Mark Sanchez, meaning certain doom for Jets fans. As the Jets spiraled out of control during the 2012 NFL season and Sanchez played poorly, she promptly ended their relationship. The girl likes winners apparently.

Recently there have been stories of guys getting in so deep with their wives or girlfriends that the relationship turns violent.

I don't understand how young wealthy athletes can act this way. Brandon Marshall is a multimillionaire wide receiver for the Miami Dolphins, and in 2011 his wife stabbed him in the stomach. She took a knife out of the kitchen drawer and stabbed him.

She went to jail for assault with a deadly weapon, and fortunately for Brandon, he survived. As soon as I heard the story, my first reaction was "How could Brandon allow this woman to get so close to him and be so in love with him that she would be driven to stab him?" You have to love somebody a lot to stab them with a kitchen knife in the stomach. The only way to be driven to that level of anger is to love someone so much you get pissed at an equal intensity when something happens.

26

GIRLS OF DENVER

I made two calls the day I got fired from CBS SportsLine. One of the first calls I made in Florida was to a guy named Rick Scott. Rick was the only sports radio consultant that I knew of in America. He had been after me for years trying to convince me to leave Philly, and later Florida, for one of many jobs he knew about for the stations he consulted.

I called him under the following premise: Being syndicated was great, but none of the stations I was on were in Florida. I missed being a part of a local community and talking about the local teams with the local fans. I wasn't lying. I also never would have called if I hadn't been fired. I understand the local fan base and play off of it, either as a rah-rah hometown guy, or by going the other way when appropriate. That's what I do best.

Rick was glad to hear from me. He suggested KKFN The Fan in Denver. He said I'd be perfect for them and told me he would call the program director there to set up a conference call. They were an AM station with the rights to the Avalanche hockey games. They had no ratings, and not a single show anybody really cared about or was passionate about.

The second call I made the day I was fired was to longtime friend Marc Lawrence. Marc is one of the foremost sports handicappers in the country. He and I had forged a close friendship when I was living in Cleveland. We had already partnered in some small businesses, and had stayed in contact throughout the years. Marc was a frequent guest on my shows. While I was at CBS SportsLine, I became familiar with an offshoot company they started called Vegas Insider. It was a website where you could buy picks from a couple of handicappers.

The problem with the site and the business in general is that the handicappers are shady. Marc Lawrence was the most honest guy I had ever met. When he lost, he told you. He never gave out both sides of the same game. He was a trend handicapper and was unwavering in using past trends to pick winners. More than that, he was a brilliant marketer: AFC Game of the Month, MLB American League Winner of the Year, and so on. Handicappers market to desperate gamblers who feel like they need an edge. If you are predisposed to gamble and you see a reputable guy who admits when he loses touting his game of the year, you will buy the information, no matter what the cost. It's like selling ice in the Sahara.

I had run my own gambling den from my parents' living room when I was in junior high school. After much nagging on my part, they bought me a video game console called Intellivision. It came loaded with a casino game, and I began playing roulette, craps, and blackjack. Soon I figured out that gambling was not only fun, but could also be an easy way to make money. I was a latchkey kid, so I started having my friends come over and play with me, betting with baseball cards, gum, anything on hand. Word spread, and kids I'd never even met started showing up at my house to gamble. I ran the casino for almost a full year. I was making serious money for a kid, and acquiring more sporting goods than I knew what to do with. When kids couldn't pay me in cash, they paid in tangible goods. I could have started my own shop.

Sadly, though, like most illegal enterprises, this business came to an abrupt end. One of the kids wagered a brand-new baseball glove, and he lost, so he left me the glove. A few days later his dad wanted to have a catch, and when his son couldn't find the glove, the dad went ballistic. The kid started to cry and ratted me out. His dad showed up at my house and told my parents what was going on. I returned the glove to the kid and then took the belt whooping of a lifetime. I never went back to Intellivision, but my love of gambling continued. I was intrigued when I learned about Vegas Insider.

I felt that Marc and I could do a better job than Vegas Insider. I called him up and explained the concept. At this point Marc had no Internet presence, and he knew he needed one. Over the course of an hour we had a tentative agreement, which we later finalized at dinner the following week.

We would build a company from scratch called Vegas Experts. Marc would supply a few things, and so would I. Marc would fund the project with a $30,000 loan. He would provide all the content for the site, and in his genius, we would guarantee all picks on the site with a pay-only-after-you-win formula. This set us apart. If you bought information on a game for $10 and the pick we gave you lost, you wouldn't have to pay for it. Your credit card would only get charged if the pick we gave you was a winner.

This was revolutionary in the industry, and it set us apart. Marc's final contribution was also ahead of its time. He knew that, like him, other handicappers had no Internet presence, either. We would bring in the top twelve most respected handicappers in the world and offer their picks on our site as well. The handicappers would give us 50 percent of their take, and we would provide them their entire Web presence for free.

I was going to run the company day-to-day, take a $3,000-a-month salary, and own 50 percent of the company with Marc. I would be responsible for building the site myself.

I had no idea how to do that, so I bought a book on programming and read it cover to cover. I built the website one page at a time from scratch during marathon eighteen-hour days. I also hired a programming friend I had met at SportsLine to do the back-end financial-transaction programming. That was far beyond the scope of what I could do as a self-taught programmer.

Five days after our dinner, we had a contract to start the business. Almost forty-five days after that, we had a website up and running, and producing income.

As I was building this company, Rick Scott and The Fan in Denver were pursuing me. It took about three weeks for me to connect with Rick and Tim Spence, the program director. Tim was impressed with my background, but he wanted me to come to Denver to meet with him and even do a show on his station so he could hear me for himself. I had sent the guy several hours of my shows and a compilation "best of" CD, which I had always hated to do. He knew what I sounded like and knew who I was, yet like a circus monkey, I would have to perform for my keep.

The problem was that I was now running a company that was starting to make money and draw interest from offshore casinos that wanted to advertise to gamblers. In theory, I could do both. I agreed to fly out to Denver and at least keep the door to radio open. I flew out to Denver on a Friday and met with Rick and Tim at a restaurant near the station. The plan was to chat on Friday, host a show on Saturday, have dinner Saturday night, and fly back to Florida on Sunday.

I walked into the restaurant and right away spotted Rick, an engaging guy, about six foot four. He gave me the man-hug with the two pats on the back and introduced me to Tim. I noticed that Tim had the largest human head I had ever seen. It was like a huge block with crazy big ears, sitting atop a freakishly small neck. I was so transfixed by his head that I had to tell myself to stop staring. I also noticed that he had no personality whatsoever—just like his radio station, apparently.

The first question from Tim: "If the Lindros situation happened here, how would you handle it with us?"

And away we go. The rest of the lunch was similarly awkward, and Rick acted as the liaison and conversation starter. After about two hours, we left. I was to do a three-hour show that night. Tim warned me that the station didn't get many calls, so I should be prepared to delve into lots of topics and do a lot of talking. How could Denver's only sports talk station not get phone calls all day and night? I didn't understand. I spent the rest of the day listening to The Fan to get a sense of what the other hosts sounded like, and what calls, if any, they did take.

What I heard was the worst sports station in America. No pizzazz, no energy, no focus; just boring rambling from a variety of different hosts who should still be studying at the Connecticut School of Broadcasting.

I went on the air at ten, about the same time that night's Rockies game ended. "Good evening. Craig Carton here on The Fan." Wow, it sounded great. Truth be told, ever since I was a kid and WFAN Radio started, I had always wanted to say that phrase. No way would I ever get to do it in New York. This was good enough for me—at least the first few times I said it. I did a three-hour show and had calls every minute of every hour. The volume of calls shocked not only Tim Spence—who later remarked, "I don't know how you did that, but I'm glad you did"—but also the show's producer, who had to answer the phone lines. Because I lived by the Bigby rule of limiting caller time, the poor guy was in over his head.

I went back to Florida the next day. I figured that if they called to hire me, I'd consider it. If not, no worries. I was building an Internet company and it was starting to do well. We had more than a thousand members, people who paid a monthly fee to get our picks at a discounted rate and to get special picks every day for them at no extra charge. We were growing at about 10 percent a week. We had effectively tapped into the degenerate world of gambling.

Over the next few weeks, I checked in with Rick Scott to see what if anything was happening with Denver. I wasn't overly concerned. I was working eighteen-hour days on the site. I didn't have time to worry about the radio opportunity.

Almost a full month later, Tim finally called.

"Craig, we would love to bring you in to do afternoons on our radio station and are prepared to make you an offer," he said.

His first proposal was such a joke, I told him no without even considering it. He wanted to sign me to a seven-month contract and pay me on a prorated basis. Mickey Mouse organization time. No thanks. If I decided to come, it would have to be for a full year with bonus incentives and option years based on success. Tim said that he needed to think about it and promised to get back to me.

I wish I'd said "Fuck off" right then and there, but I didn't. It took

Tim three days to call me back, which was another sign I should have considered when deciding whether to take the job. Ultimately they offered me $67,500 and bonuses for being one of the top-five-rated shows in my time slot that could have added another $25,000 to my base. I told him I would consider it and get back to him by the next day.

I called Marc Lawrence to let him know I had the offer, and that if I took it, I would move our company to Denver and run it from there when I wasn't on the air. We had hired two employees to deal with customer service, and I figured that if there were any other pressing issues, I could handle them before and after the show. I also wasn't done with radio in my heart. I was pissed at how SportsLine came to an end, and I didn't want that to be the final story of my career. I wanted to go out on top and prove to all the naysayers that I was successful.

Marc didn't love the idea, nor should he have. We were building a company that had his name attached to it. But I had delivered on my guarantees and promises, and he and I had an open and long-standing relationship. He wished me well and told me he trusted me to always do the right thing.

I called Tim Spence and accepted the job. One week after I started, I wished I never had. Not because I didn't love doing radio. I love radio—even though at times I was bored and not challenged by it unlike now. But I regretted agreeing to work for Tim. In my radio career I had only worked for one truly incompetent PD, and that was Charlie Barker in Florida. Tim was the second. Tim was big on meeting right before and right after every single show. He loved to stifle any and all organic entertainment.

•   •   •

I knew I had to make my mark in Denver as soon as possible, and I knew that I would stand out from the other hosts in town. I had never done nor wanted to do straight X's-and-O's sports talk. At WIP I had learned how to do a good show. Now I just had to learn which sports Denver fans cared most about and add the guy mix. I figured I was all set.

The first thing I did, even before my initial air shift, was to go to the top two strip clubs in Denver and introduce myself to the managers. I told them that I wanted to highlight their clubs by bringing one of the girls in each week to play a sports game with me. Strip club managers never say no to a free promotion. The ulterior motive, of course, was that I would get to meet all the top strippers in town. Even better, I would meet them as the guy on the radio, not as some schmuck begging for a lap dance.

My plan worked right away. I had been on the air for a month when the station had a pregame appearance at an Avalanche game. I was the new afternoon guy and figured nobody knew me. The other hosts had all been there for at least a full year, if not more. I showed up a few minutes after them and made my way to the station tent. Within a few minutes, guys mobbed me, asking if I was the new guy on the radio with all the hot chicks. Nobody knew what I had said about the local teams. They just knew that I was the guy with the sexy girls who played games. The president of distribution of a beer company, whose corporate office was in Denver, invited me to sit with him in his box for the game. He, too, only wanted to hear about all the hot women.

One month, and that's all it took. I was killing it in Denver. Through the strip clubs I met a photographer doing a "Girls of Denver" shoot for *Playboy*. He was going to shuttle some of the girls my way to promote the magazine and hook me up. The most memorable of all these women was named Susan. She was maybe twenty-two. Her voice was like candy, and she sounded like the most erotic stripper you'd ever met. I later had her come to the studio. She had platinum blond hair, big fake boobs, and a forty-five-year-old husband who looked like a stoner.

I eventually became friends with Susan and her husband, Bob, and started to socialize with them. Now, I admit, I'm not the best at keeping in touch with people, and I suck at intimacy, but as a surface-type friend to party with, I am your man. That's what we did, until things went south.

Susan and Bob liked to party from time to time. When they did, he became jealous of guys hitting on Susan, which of course always happened. And then she would become enraged at him for not trusting her. One night they were partying and in the middle of a huge fight, and driving home on the highway, according to both of them, Susan decided to punch him in the face, almost causing him to drive off the road. He retaliated by calling her a skanky whore and demanded to know how many dicks she was sucking behind his back. She then called him "a limp-dicked, big-bellied old man." He kicked her out of the car and told her to walk the rest of the way. When she got home, she called the police, and things escalated. I was unaware of all this until my phone rang that night. It was Bob. The police had been over, Susan had walked out, and he was alone and wanted to die.

Halfheartedly I asked him what he meant about wanting to die, and he said he was going to kill himself and needed me to come over to talk him down. Life lesson number one for Bob: He called the wrong guy. I knew him socially but didn't know him that well. There had to be someone else he could have called to tell that he was going to kill himself. I engaged him for about a half hour and made it clear that a) I wasn't coming over, and b) killing himself would be stupid. I suggested that he go to bed and call me in the morning. If he was still depressed, I would come over. What a great friend I was.

They got back together, as she had nowhere to live and he wasn't going to land another hot twenty-two-year-old. The crisis was averted. When my future wife flew to visit me, I told her that my best friend in Denver would pick her up at the airport and spend the day with her since I had to work. That was Susan, and what a great introduction to the town for my wife. Hi, I'm a stripper with big boobs who knows your soon-to-be husband. Let's hang out for the day. Oh, and by the way, I swear I never fucked him.

My show soon became the number-one show on the radio station and the highest-rated in the station's history—and I hated it. I had started to refuse to go to pre-show meetings, and only took post-show meetings when Spence cornered me. Besides the distraction of his big head, he liked to talk in parables and metaphors. After one of my strip-per shows resulted in the girl being naked and doing jumping jacks for Broncos tickets, he said to me, "Craig, you are building a house and it's a nice house, but today you burned down the deck. Why did you burn the deck down?" I had no fucking idea what he was talking about, but I knew I needed to leave.

They moved my time slot a few times in the first nine months to try to have my audience cover both middays and some afternoon real estate to help the ratings for the entire station. Then they thought I should do mornings—something I didn't want to do. Having established myself in the early afternoon, I knew how hard it would be to then build an audience in a different time slot. I had established something great and didn't want to mess with it. I couldn't guarantee that the quick success I'd had would transfer to mornings. KKFN was a lousy station, and I was happy doing my thing right where I was for the time being.

Once a week, my afternoon show was live from a bar in Larimer

Square in downtown Denver. The show attracted crowds of nearly a thousand people. It became a must-attend event. I decided to make it a circus-like show and brought in local celebrities, athletes, and girls. I gave the crowd an awesome four hours of entertainment. To this day, the events are some of the best pure entertainment shows I ever did. What I did not know was that the huge crowds also brought an important visitor to the bar every week. He came alone the first three weeks, and he came with his boss the last week. I was being watched, but I didn't know it.

Just before Bob Richards came and changed my life in Denver, something far more serious did. For a few months, I had a strange sensation in my arm, making it feel extremely tight. My fingers tingled, and at times my arm looked bloated and purple. I did nothing about it until I complained about it during one of the live shows, and medics came to check me out. They couldn't figure it out, either, but suggested I have it MRI'd. I did, and again, nothing. I wasn't too concerned, but it was in the back of my mind.

One day I went to the gym to work out, and I couldn't even lift the bar with no weight on it. After work that day, instead of going home, I checked my voice mail. There was a message from Dr. Michael Cooper's office. He was a top thoracic specialist and worked out of Swedish Memorial Hospital. The message was that he could see me that day at 4 p.m. if I wanted. Otherwise, it was going to be a month until he had an opening.

I called Kim, who'd moved to Denver three days earlier, and told her I was going to go, then I'd swing by the house and pick her up for dinner. I walked into his office and he asked me to take my shirt off and raise my hands as if I were under arrest. I did, and within ten seconds, he said, "You're going to the hospital and right to the ICU. You have a blood clot, and it needs attention immediately." Stunned and bewildered, I signed a bunch of papers, got directions, and left. I called Kim and told her to be ready, but not for dinner. We were going to the hospital.

I had thoracic outlet syndrome, and had a blood clot the size of small cigar a few inches from my heart. TOS is when the clavicle and a rib push against the muscles, arteries, and veins and cut off the blood supply to the arm and fingers. The doctor would have to remove my first rib, take out the clot and the bad vein, and take a healthy vein from my ankle to repair the bad one. I was also going to be on aggressive blood thinners—and oh, by the way, I could die.

I went to the hospital, filled out more paperwork, was admitted to the ICU, and within an hour I was hooked up to a shitload of machines and wires. They were going to do a venogram to locate the clot and then prepare for surgery the next morning.

A young nurse tried seventeen times to get a blood line going before the doctor showed up and stopped her. A few hours before the surgery, a priest came to my room to talk. I told him I was not a big God guy, and I was Jewish. He counseled me that I should talk to someone, and that he would send a rabbi in. Even though they were coming because the surgery could go wrong and I could die, I never considered dying. A few minutes later, the rabbi showed up, and I dismissed him as well, but I thanked him for coming in. I was on my own. God would not be in the room this time.

The surgery went perfectly. My rib was taken out, I survived, and I recovered for two days in a private section of the hospital. The only drawback to the operation was that when I woke up, my groin hurt more than the area of the surgery. They neglected to tell me that I would be catheterized, and that they took a vein from my groin as opposed to my ankle. I had a tube going inside my penis. I was miserable. I needed it out.

The sweet, sympathetic nurse said to me, "Here's the deal: if I take it out, you have thirty minutes to pee on your own. If you don't, I'm putting it back in without anesthesia." I kicked everybody out of the room and had the nurse turn the water on, but no luck. I called Kim back in and had her make a hissing noise like a snake in my ear. Again, no luck. I then had her bring warm water for me to dip my hands in. No luck. The clock was ticking. It was twenty-nine minutes in when I dripped a few drops of urine. Thank God, because the nurse had a weird smile as she prepared the catheter for my small, scared penis. I was home free, or so I thought.

Then celebrity hit again.

Norm Clarke, the popular gossip writer in Vegas who was a friend of mine, had written about my predicament. When I started to come to in my room after the surgery, I saw Kim and my folks, and there were two other people I didn't recognize. Neither did anybody else, but no one had the wherewithal to ask them who they were. "I know I'm fucked-up on drugs, but who are you guys?" I asked. I was hoping they were friends, and I was so messed up on morphine, that I just forgot who they were. It turned out they were fans of the show, read Norm's column, and showed up to bring me food and gifts. Awkward. I thanked them, and hospital staffers asked them to leave. Norm then got pissed at me because I never thanked him for writing about my health issues. Unreal!

I would miss one week of work for the first time in my career, but I was set to come back on April 20, 1999. I returned to the show with Dave Otto, and we broadcast live from a supermarket five miles outside Littleton, Colorado. Most of the show was about my return and some baseball nonsense, too. All was fine until two fucked-up kids decided to open fire on innocent students at Littleton's Columbine High School. That was my first day back on the air. It is a day I will never forget. It is also a day I don't want to remember.

•　　•　　•

It turned out that the guy who had come to my Larimer Square events was Bob Richards. He was the program director of a legendary rock station in Denver, 106.7: KBPI Rocks the Rockies. I knew Bob from Buffalo. He ran the rock station there when I was just getting started at WGR. We didn't know each other well, but we had met. Bob waited until a full hour after the show, when most of the people other than those looking to party the rest of the day with me had cleared out.

As he approached, I recognized him. We shook hands, and he asked if he could buy me a drink. The answer to that question is always "yes." We sat on the outside deck of the bar, and he told me that he was running KBPI, which I didn't know. They were huge fans of mine and couldn't believe the crowds or the ratings I was getting at the dump I was working at. He wanted to know my contract status, and if I wanted to do mornings for them.

My contract had only a few months left and I wanted out, so that would not be a problem, I thought. And yes, I would love to work there. It was a perfect place for what I was creating in Denver: a hardcore, young, male-skewing rock station. Most of their daytime shows did well, but they had a lousy morning show, and that was holding the station back from reaching its true potential. Assuming we could work out a deal, he wanted me to start the first Tuesday in October, so they could maximize my arrival for the fall ratings period.

I wanted out of my FAN contract. I had recently been moved to doing the morning drive, and while I didn't mind getting up, they gave me a partner named Dave Otto. I liked Dave, but I went from being a number-one hot solo show to having a partner and needing to incorporate him into the show. Dave was a radio vet, and he understood what I did, so we got along from jump-street. But I was not doing the show I wanted to do anymore, and I was pissed. There was no raise in the move, and no assurance of anything in the future, plus with daily meetings and being there at 6 a.m., I was tired and miserable.

We were preparing for the biggest promotion of the year, which involved me and Dave going on the road for a week. I decided to schedule my wedding for the same week, pretending that I didn't know the actual dates. The promotion was called "Germany" because we were going to fly to Germany and broadcast our show live from there to celebrate BeerFest. I waited a few days, and then I told Tim that I needed a few days off to get married—but not to worry; I wouldn't take a full honeymoon and compromise the fall ratings.

When he saw the date, his first reaction was priceless. Rather than say congrats, he said, "Oh, I didn't give you permission to get married on that day." Fuck you. Sorry, I'm getting married and I can't go to Germany. It shocked him, and I loved every minute of it. I thought he was a micromanager and had no appreciation for good radio. He once even sent me a rejection letter for a job after I was already working there. He was a disorganized leader. Even though he had been given the power to run the station, I felt that he lacked the ability to do the job. Screw him!

It took all of twenty-four hours for him and the station GM to call me into a meeting. I was expecting it, and so was Bob at KBPI. We had agreed on a one-year deal for $70,000 plus bonuses. I would be the main host of the KBPI morning show, which would be called *The Locker Room*.

Tim and the GM told me they were letting me go due to creative differences, and they would pay out the rest of my contract if I agreed not to sue for wrongful termination. I signed, went home, and called Bob. Nine minutes later, Bob faxed me a contract and I had a deal. Nine minutes of unemployment, and I would double-dip a salary for the first sixty days.

I did get married, and did keep my word about a two-day Vegas honeymoon. I started the first Monday of October as the host of *The Locker Room* on KBPI. I was pumped.

Then reality hit, as it so often does. When I was about three or four months into the job my wife and I found out she was pregnant. I was loving the station and the gig, and to celebrate my arrival, I organized a huge giveaway. I was going to drop the station van from a helicopter one thousand feet in the air onto an old dirt raceway field. The field would be sectioned off into huge boxes, each of which would have a number. Whatever listener had the rights to the numbered box that the van fell on would win a brand-new van. I also encouraged listeners to bring their own vehicles to be dropped from the helicopter.

With no expectations whatsoever, we did the on-air box giveaway for two weeks, and then went out to the field on a Saturday. Nearly ten thousand people showed up to try to win the van. The station had been rocking the Rockies for decades, and in a matter of weeks, I had contrived and pulled off the biggest promotion that it ever had.

But two months later I left Denver.

Without getting into specifics, my wife's pregnancy wasn't the easiest, and I knew I had to get her back to the East Coast. I waited for the first rating period to come, to see how we did. In three months, we were the number-one morning show in every key male demographic. The station was thrilled; it made Bob look great because I had delivered on my promise. It was the beginning of what could have been a legendary Denver career.

At the same time, I was running out of hours in the day to run the Internet company. I called Marc right when the KBPI job started and told him I would sell him my shares, act as a consultant for six months to train his guys on how to do what I did, and devote myself 100 percent to radio. I could not do both. Marc agreed to buy me out of the company. As much as I thought I let him down, sixty days later he signed a lucrative marketing deal with an offshore sports book that would be the title sponsor of the site. The site had grown to be the most-trafficked sports handicapping website in the world.

I didn't get a single nickel of the marketing deal money, so while I wasn't the best businessman when it came to timing, I am still proud of what I built. The site still exists, and it is still profitable. Marc has since sold out. He and I started another venture soon after, and we remain close friends.

When the ratings came in at KBPI for my third ratings book, we were number one again. It wasn't two weeks later that I had to go to Bob Richards and tell him I was resigning. He was crushed. "Is it about the money for the show?" he asked. I told him I would never do that. I always honored a contract I'd signed, but it was nice to know he could have paid me more than he did. When I told him why I had to leave and that I would give him as much notice as possible, he hugged me and said, "There's nothing I can do to change your mind, since you are doing it for family reasons. Let's call it over at the end of the week."

I told him I would regret the decision the day I walked out the door, never to return. He asked that I not announce it on the radio. This was hard for me because I had built a great relationship with the audience and felt a sense of duty to tell them. But I kept my promise and disappeared without a word.

I did my last show, packed up my house, and drove from Denver to the East Coast with a pregnant wife, two dogs, and unfulfilled dreams. We decided to move back to Philadelphia. My wife was from Philly, and having her family around seemed like a good idea. I was miserable about leaving Denver. I had moved there to resurrect my radio career and give it one last shot. As a result I sold Vegas Experts, a business I loved. I had built it from scratch and watched it succeed, and now here I was, about to become a father for the first time, and I was unemployed.

I had sold my shares in VE for a good chunk of change, but not enough to live on forever without any other income. I had to get back to work. I decided to build another Internet company, and to keep my hands in radio.

From the radio perspective, I was in Philly, so I called Bigby and told him I was back. He told me he wanted me back full-time. Middays would be mine. Ha; I'd heard that one before, but this time I didn't have any interest in being the midday guy at WIP. The best time slot is morning drive (6–10 a.m.), followed by the afternoon drive (3–7 p.m.). I had proven to be a number-one morning show host, and if I was going to get back into radio full-time, I wasn't going to be talking sports at WIP from 10 a.m. to 1 p.m. I agreed to host the Brian Mitchell show. Brian was the new return man for the Eagles. Every Monday night he was going to have a two-hour radio show from a local sports bar, and I would host it. I told Bigby that I would also be willing to fill in for other day parts occasionally.

In my free time, I started an Internet company, Calling Stars. When I was building and running Vegas Experts, I developed and had exclusive rights to a new technology that would allow users to click a button on a website and initiate a phone call to whatever number they entered. The phone call would be a recorded message, and could be timed to coincide with a multimedia message on the computer screen. The original idea was that gamblers could have top handicappers "call" them to give them their picks, and if they were in front of their computers, they could also see the trends the handicappers were referencing when they explained why a certain team would be a pick that day.

When I got to Denver, I shared the technology with a company called CTS. They demonstrated the technology by releasing a website called Call Me Santa. This site allowed kids to get a call from Santa during Christmas and watch as Santa got the sleigh and reindeer ready to deliver presents. More than a million people initiated the call from Santa, and thus we had proven the technology and concept.

My idea was to sign up athletes and entertainers with Calling Stars so that fans could pay a couple of dollars to get birthday calls, well wishes, and personal updates from their favorite stars. I had signed about six athletes or so and had developed a contact with the manager of 'N Sync, the hottest boy band in the world at the time.

I spent most days trying to build the business and sign deals with celebrities. Then I decided that one of the coolest applications of the technology would be to incorporate it into video games. Having trouble with level three on Tomb Raider? Why not have Lara Croft call you herself to walk you through the level? I produced a demo of how it would work, with a complete multimedia presentation. I flew to San Francisco and met with the top gaming companies in America. The opportunity to bring their characters to life in this manner enticed them. When I walked out of the first meeting, I left with a verbal agreement to do a single trial run for the newest Tomb Raider game, and a request from three other game makers to produce demos for them, too. I also had a date for a second meeting. I felt great about the prospects and got to work making demos for three new games.

At the same time, I decided that another great application for Calling Stars was adult entertainment. I hired two young, attractive models and had them record sexy messages in which they described doing certain things such as getting undressed or massaging themselves. Soft porn at its best. I sent the demo to Vivid Entertainment, the largest producer of adult entertainment videos in America, and also to Flynt Productions.

Both companies loved the idea, and their respective directors of new business development asked me to fly out to Hollywood. I met with Vivid first. They were based in a nondescript one-story warehouse, not impressive when you considered that they sold millions of dollars' worth of videos and sex toys every single year. They understood the concept and wanted to produce one with Jenna Jameson, the hottest porn actress on the planet at the time. We wrote a two-minute script for Jenna. She would tape the corresponding sex scenes to go along with the audio. Home run.

From Vivid, I drove to to meet with Larry Flynt's son, who was running all of his father's digital properties. It was one of the most fascinating offices I have ever been in, and not sleazy at all. It was a professional building with amazing art on the walls and not a single naked woman anywhere in sight. I had dreams of the Flynt building being a nonstop Hefner-style party. But these guys ran a business, and acted that way. Flynt was accommodating, and like everyone else, he saw how the application of the technology could be a real winner.

I housed the technology on my servers, so companies that wanted to use it had no cost at all and no bandwidth issues. Their only cost was whatever they had to pay their talent to do recordings and performances. I had planned that rather than license them the technology, I would do a profit split. My feeling was that people go to these companies every day asking for money, and I would be different. If I showed them that they could improve their Web presence, and bring in significant revenue with no cost at all, I was ahead of anyone else who would meet with them that day. Flynt liked the idea so much that he took me to the Hustler store to get some stuff for my wife, and then out for drinks. I was about to become a porn mogul.

I flew back to Philly to share the good news and to host the Brian Mitchell show. I had lost interest in the show because I didn't care if the Eagles won or lost, and other than wanting Brian to do well, I didn't have any interest in his stats. The show was predictable: I would ask Brian a few questions about the game, and then I'd act as a traffic cop for callers who wanted to talk to him about the game. Every caller for those types of shows is the same: "Hey, Brian. Great game, I'm a big fan. Hey, what happened on third-and-six in the first quarter?" That kind of mindless banter bores the hell out of me.

After the show, I was approached by a man who introduced himself as Jeff Hillery. Jeff had just left a job as a program director at a FM talk station in Philly and was starting one in Dallas. He had loved me when I was at WIP and really enjoyed the Brian Mitchell show. We went for a drink, and he told me that he wanted me to be his afternoon guy in Dallas. Here we go again.

I was on the verge of major business and revenue for Calling Stars, but again I thought I could do both. I told him if the offer was right, I would consider it. He said that it would be a six-figure deal per year, for three years. My daughter, Mickey J., had been born in 2000, and the baby and my wife were doing well. I had no real reason not to consider taking the job and moving. Hillery also said I could bring any producer I wanted, and do whatever kind of show I wanted. This arrangement was new to me, and I was intrigued.

After discussing it with my wife, I figured why not. I called Jeff and told him we had a deal, and to fax it over to me. The last fax offer I got took nine minutes in Denver. Jeff told me he was going to his fax machine right now, and the fax would be coming in thirty seconds. He went on and on about how successful we would be.

I went online looking at houses and doing neighborhood research on suburban Dallas. Five minutes had passed, and the fax didn't come. I checked the phone line, waited another ten minutes, and still no fax. I called Jeff and got his voice mail. Thirty minutes, nothing; an hour, nothing; voice mail, nothing, nothing. I still have not gotten that fax.

I have never spoken to Jeff Hillery since he last told me we had a deal and was faxing me a contract. I was pissed—not because I wasn't going to Dallas, but pissed that he would play me the way he did without ever calling me back or explaining what the fuck happened.

I went back to working part-time at WIP and building Calling Stars. For the Internet venture, I signed John Valentin, the starting third baseman of the Boston Red Sox; Adam Deadmarsh of the Colorado Avalanche; and Rob Ray of the Buffalo Sabres. I had ten more pending contracts with athletes nationwide.

Then I met with the representatives of 'N Sync. This deal was the potential grand slam. While the athletes would bring in core fans of their respective teams, if I could get Justin Timberlake and the gang to record nothing more than an 'N Sync rendition of "Happy Birthday," Calling Stars would make millions. Their reps loved the concept and told me they would need a week to present me with a proposal of what they would need. They had to protect the band's interests and be careful about who they went into business with.

During the week that they were thinking about it, I kept plugging away and, as I am still wont to do, I checked out a few radio rumor websites. One day I saw a blurb that Scott Kaplan had been fired as cohost of *The Drive*. The same show that he and Sid Rosenberg had done alongside me at CBS SportsLine had somehow been picked up and aired in New York City by WNEW Radio.

That one decision alone is proof that radio executives have no idea what they are doing sometimes. It was an awful show with no energy at all, and if Scott had half the talent he did ego, it may have had a shot. He didn't, yet I'm sure it wasn't all his fault. Sid was a degenerate gambler, a drug addict, and an alcoholic. He was incredibly engaging and talented, and people generally liked him despite his problems and his ability to lie right to your face. I felt that way about Sid.

On a whim, I sent a package up to Jeremy Coleman, the program director of WNEW. As I put it into the overnight bin, the most amazing feeling came over me. I knew I was going to be offered the job to replace Scott. It's the only time in my life I have ever experienced that kind of premonition.

The following Monday, I was driving to the sports bar outside of Philly to host the Brian Mitchell show when my cell phone rang. It was Jeremy Coleman. He wanted to chat. I pulled over to the side of the road and we talked for twenty minutes about the radio station, the show, and about me. He wanted me to do some tryout shows with Sid. I magically enrolled my sister in New York University and told him I would be up there on Thursday. If that worked, I could do the shows on Thursday and Friday. Not having a good reason to say no, he said okay.

Wednesday afternoon I drove up to New York and crashed at a buddy's apartment to get ready to be at WNEW on Thursday morning. At the time, WNEW had one extremely successful show, *Opie & Anthony*. The Radio Chick did middays, and the morning show was now going to be called *The Sports Guys*. Sid Rosenberg was there, as was comedian Eddie Ifft, former football player John Riggins once a week, Billy Taylor once a week, and a parade of others. In other words, they didn't have a show. The first person I met in the waiting room was the board op (the guy who pushes the buttons that play commercials, songs, sounds, etc.), and assistant producer Chris Oliviero, or "Olive," as I called him. I then met Mattie Moonshine, the producer, and Sid, who came in with a huge bear hug and told me how happy he was to see me. I did the two tryout shows, and based on my background and the fact that no one on the show had done radio really, they had me go to the calls and do the radio shit. I did my usual mix-it-up-with-the-callers banter, hung up on some of them, and kept the show moving like I had done thousands of times before.

Mattie told me I was exactly what they needed, and he would recommend that I get the gig. Jeremy Coleman, who also had no background in programming but was a nice guy, even though he was in over his head and had no control over the shows, called me into his office and told me how much he enjoyed hearing me. He wanted to offer me the job.

Holy shit. I was going to be doing mornings in New York City, and going up against Howard Stern, Scott Shannon, and all the other stations I grew up listening to. Jeremy asked how much I cost. I threw a random number out there and said well above what I had ever made before. He said no problem. You start next Monday.

Fuck, I should have asked for more than that. Actually, you know how some ballplayers say they would play for free? I would have done mornings in New York for free at that moment, for sure. Little did I know I was walking into one of the least professional radio stations in America.

The station promoted itself as the Opie & Anthony Station. That was really the only show that mattered, and the only show that would be promoted. This scenario could be good or bad, depending on your perspective. Good that we could fly under the radar and build a show, bad because we would get no support whatsoever to build it.

Here I was in New York, the number-one media market in the world and the home of the some of the greatest radio personalities since Marconi invented the medium. Yet when I looked around the studio at the collection of "talent" I would be working with, none of them had any real history of being successful on-air. Eddie Ifft was a comedian who had never done radio before the WNEW gig. Billy Taylor was a former NFL player who had been a guest on radio shows, but never hosted one. John Riggins, same deal. Blain Ensley was the on-air producer of a successful show but never had the desire or the experience in having to help carry a show on the air. Other than enjoying listening to WFAN, Sid Rosenberg had been on the air on a real radio show for less than eighteen months.

But I didn't really care. I was just happy to be on the air in my hometown and doing mornings. I did have this other issue, though, and that was Calling Stars. Thank God for greed and dubious businesspeople. When I called to follow up with the 'N Sync people, they told me they would need a guarantee of $1 million, and they would only do one recording. I didn't care about that one recording, because "Happy Birthday" was all I cared about, but there was no way I could guarantee the million, and they knew it. I told them I would get back to them by week's end with an answer and a contract for them to review. What happened next, though, shocked even me.

Before we ever got to the end of the week, 'N Sync made a major announcement. They had signed an agreement with a company that had the same type of technology, and it was supported by a major national bank. They took my idea, went to a competing company, and used the exact same idea I had pitched them on a month earlier. Fucking assholes. But the best part was that the idea never worked, and other than whatever money they got from the title sponsor, people never went for the phone call to their homes from 'N Sync. I dodged a bullet. Now I was exclusively a radio guy. Having learned from my experience with Vegas Experts, I decided to drop the Calling Stars idea and concentrate on radio. I figured this was my only shot to make it in New York, and I was going to give it all of my attention. I called the athletes I had signed up to the company, explained to them that I was moving on, and closed the Calling Stars chapter then and there.

Let the games begin.

The Sports Guys show had no shot. Not only did nobody care about us; the show itself stunk. Sid only wanted to be a straight sports guy, and only wanted to be on WFAN Radio. Sid adored the FAN, as did most New York kids who loved sports and made WFAN listening a daily ritual. His screen saver was a picture of WFAN host Chris "Mad Dog" Russo, and once Sid got on the air as a broadcaster, his main goal was to work at WFAN. It was as if Sid thought that if he could get to WFAN, it would legitimize him as a radio talent. Sid knows as much as anyone who has ever worked at WFAN, and it's a shame that his personal demons robbed of him what would have been a very lucrative career.

Sid hated the guy talk stuff, boycotted most of it, and really wanted to be taken seriously as a sports guy. He knew his shit, no doubt about that, but I didn't think straight sports would ever garner ratings, especially on a hard-core guys' station with *Opie & Anthony* as the afternoon show.

The other issue, aside from Sid and I not agreeing on what to talk about every day, was that Jeremy Coleman wasn't a New Yorker or a sports fan—nor, for that matter, was he a good programmer. And on top of that, Sid spent as much time worrying about who was after him as he did working on doing a good radio show—drug dealers, bookies, whoever. He spent countless hours crying by the elevator, hoping people weren't waiting for him to kill him. He came to work many times with black eyes or incredible stories of how he ducked someone who was looking for him.

I spent countless hours bemoaning that we had an incredible opportunity but it was being flushed down the drain. We had no ratings at all, and the ratings we did have got worse when ESPN broadcast their newest show with Michael Wilbon and Tony Kornheiser called

PTI—or *Pardon the Interruption.* This show was new, and one-of-a-kind. It changed how TV sports are presented forever. As a team, Wilbon and Kornheiser are great. What they have is much like the natural rapport that I am blessed to have with Boomer. It's a bond, and a relationship that cannot be manufactured. Abbott and Costello had it, but Abbott and anyone else would have been a disaster. Partners either have it, or they do not.

The problem for me was that Jeremy Coleman only knew ESPN when it came to sports. He figured if they were doing it on TV, we should do it on the radio. That year, 2001, the Yankees were making a run to the postseason again, and they dominated the headlines. But Jeremy had decided that we would do a radio version of *PTI,* something he called the Mad Minute. His idea was to change the topic every ten minutes, no matter what. Yankees win the World Series? You did ten minutes on it. Fuck off, now talk about something else. Olive and I tried to explain why that was a bad idea, but Jeremy didn't care. He sent us a memo about how to get better ratings, and the only thing on the list was

1: Do better show.

Yet he was hamstringing us.

The souring of a thousand and one things between Sid and me was bad. He had given up on trying to do a good show. His demons had gotten to him, and he had to disappear for a while. He decided to go to Florida for Passover. Nothing wrong with that, but he went to Florida without telling anyone, and then once he was there, he told Jeremy that he needed at least a week to celebrate his Judaism. Jeremy wasn't Jewish and he didn't know any better, but our assistant PD was Jewish, and he knew it was bullshit right away. By this point, Sid owed half the building money. Management was tired of his act. Given our show's ratings, they called Sid up and told him to stay in Florida and not bother coming back. He was fired. Of course, Sid blamed me for it, but I had nothing to do with it. I was taking a nap when our producer called me to tell me I would be on alone the next morning because Sid was fired.

Blain Ensley, the former cohost producer of the Rocky Allen show on WPLJ and WABC, replaced Sid. I loved Blain, but he wasn't an on-air guy, and he didn't want to be. I was fucked even more.

We did the best show we could, and he was a great partner. The show just never caught on, and with so many moving pieces over more than a year, how could it have? Labor Day came, and I had six months left on my deal. I knew I wasn't going to be renewed. My goal was to do the best shows I could and hope to make a showing in the fall book so that I could land a Top 5 market gig elsewhere. CBS liked me, so it wasn't out of the question.

Blain and I started the first Monday of the football season, talking Jets and the pending Monday night game for the New York Giants against the Denver Broncos. Our studio was on Fifty-Sixth Street and Seventh Avenue. I sat across from our board operator, although a huge desk-like console separated us. I faced the computers. Olive had the radio board, a computer, and two televisions on in front of him. Blain sat to my right with one computer. The call screener and associate producer sat outside our studio and communicated to Olive via instant message, or they would come into the studio if it was urgent.

Monday night, Blain and I had an appearance at a sports bar to watch the Giants-Broncos game. About twenty-five people showed up. We got paid and went home. Tuesday morning, we started the show talking about the Giants loss. The show was moving along great, we were taking calls, and it felt like we had a good morning show going.

More than an hour into the show, I noticed that Olive's attention was being taken by something on TV. Olive was the most professional guy I had ever worked with, and for him to be distracted, I knew that something was up.

I asked him on the air what he was looking at. He said it looked like a plane had flown into the World Trade Center.

It was September 11, 2001.

No reason to walk through every aspect of that day in this book, but that day is the most tragic radio show I have ever done. Not a day goes by when I don't think about the countless people who called me on the radio as the last thing they ever did before the buildings came down. We told everyone who called to hang up and get out. None of them could, of course.

We stayed on the air for an extra hour or so before Don and Mike came on for the midday show. I walked from Fifty-Sixth and Seventh to Eighty-Sixth and Broadway, where my wife and only child at the time were. We went to the roof and stared in silence for most of the rest of the day.

TWO months later, with ratings still lagging, Jeremy asked me and Blain to meet with Scott Ferrall. He told us they were considering Scott to work with us. I have always liked Scott and his show. He was the most perfect nighttime host I had ever heard. Great voice for it, great demeanor, great relationship with the young audience, and great energy. Mel Karmazin, the president of Infinity, was going to make Scott a big star, and that process was under way when Scott followed his passion of doing NHL play-by-play. He was much more suited for the talk show world, though. His hockey stint was brief.

We met with Scott, and he started off by giving Blain and me a bottle of Scotch. Then he went into one of most impressive forty-minute rants I have ever witnessed. He didn't sit down once, and he didn't stop talking. Jeremy, Blain, and I didn't say a word. When he was done, we shook hands and that was it. Jeremy told me that he wanted Scott to come in to do a two-minute rant at the top of every hour, and then leave the studio until the next rant.

I hated the idea. You can't bottle up a guy like Scott for fifty-eight minutes, keep him out of the studio, and then bring him in to shoot his load within two minutes, and then make him leave again. I suggested that we make him a full cohost of the show, and the three of us would go for it. Blain preferred creating packaged bits anyhow, so Scott and I could host the show together.

Jeremy said he would consider it, and he told me that he left Scott with strict orders not to say anything about it. I was cool with Ferrall joining us, and thought it would extend the life of the show at least six months and give us another shot.

We never got that shot. The next day while he was hosting the Eagles pregame show in Philly at WYSP with Jody McDonald, Ferrall went on the air and said he was the new host of the WNEW morning show, and he was going to save the day. Of course, he said that in Ferralldelphia. WYSP is a CBS-owned station, and calls were made to Jeremy, who was pissed at the leak from Ferrall. Ferrall, told he couldn't be trusted, wasn't getting the job.

Three months later we had the station Christmas party, and everyone was fake and celebratory about the show. I wasn't going to go to the party, but I figured it would be in bad taste if I didn't. Jeremy, Opie, and station GM Ken Stevens acted as if everything were grand.

The following Monday, they told me that my contract wasn't going to be renewed, and best of luck. The only good news was that I would get paid until June 1 as a parting gift for my troubles. The day after I walked out the door, Scott Ferrall walked in. He and Blain were the new morning show. I later found out that Tom Bigby made the ultimate decision. He was now consulting with Jeremy. The show lasted less than a year and was canceled, as was the entire talk format months later.

I decided to enjoy some time off with my wife and daughter before deciding what I would do next.

I had no idea that "next" meant having my life threatened by a sitting governor, being offered Howard Stern's job, and becoming the most listened-to afternoon radio host in America. Not to mention becoming the highest-rated morning show back in New York City, and replacing a legend at the station where my journey began twenty years earlier as an intern.

We moved back to Philadelphia, and once again I was being paid to be unemployed. I contemplated lots of different business ideas, including opening up a new restaurant, but all I wanted was another radio gig. About three weeks after we moved, my phone rang. It was Eric Johnson, the program director of WKXW, better known as New Jersey 101.5 Radio. Eric was Tom Bigby's assistant program director for a few years while I was at WIP, so we knew each other. I knew he was running the station, but I had no idea what the station was all about.

As it turned out, NJ 101.5 was interesting. You could hear it all the way to Manhattan. It came in to Philly loud and clear with a great FM signal. Eric told me that there might be an opening for nights, and he wanted to know if I was free to do some fill-in shows for them while their afternoon show was on vacation. Seeing as how I had nothing else to do, I said I would be happy to come by.

I went into the station on a Thursday and bumped into hosts of the afternoon show, Scott and Casey, two of the least talented guys in the history of radio. I would be filling in for them while they were away.

Even Dennis Malloy, the cohost of the midday show, when he found out that they had been approached about doing a radio show in Detroit, commented: "Someone heard their show and offered them a job in radio? Shocking!"

Anyhow, I knew the drill by this time. I did a Thursday show without a problem. Then I decided to leave them with a lasting memory on Friday. I told a story on-air about how I saw a baby locked in a car in a Jersey mall parking lot, and when the parent of the baby came out of the store thirty minutes later, with me sitting by the car to make sure the baby was safe, she yelled at me for intruding into her business. On and on I went.

People reacted as you might think they would, with despair, anger, and unfettered emotion. Then the coup de grace: the Newark *Star-Ledger* called and wanted to interview me. I got the call from Eric Johnson after I had left for the day and told him I didn't want any more attention. The station could take credit and respond however they liked. I had made my impression, and left them wanting more.

On Monday, Eric called and asked if I could come in and meet with the GM, Andy Santoro. Andy was about five foot seven with a small belly. He could have been right out of *Goodfellas* casting. He was also a huge fan of mine from my WNEW days, and was enamored with New York radio, and more specifically, WFAN. I had him at hello.

Eric talked to me about doing nights and asked if I would sign a two-year contract to be his full-time evening host. I had grander plans and did not want to be tied to the station for two years, especially if I would only be doing nights. I explained to Eric that I would do nights, but without a contract to tie me down. I promised that I would give them two weeks' notice if I received an offer from some other radio station. Luckily for me, Andy Santoro had wanted me for afternoons all along, so the night idea never became an issue.

Then Andy took over and said, "Eric, why even float that? Craig is a major market talent. He isn't doing nights. Craig, we want you for afternoons." Bang, just like that I learned 1) Andy was the guy to go to for all decisions, and 2) Eric Johnson was a paper-pusher with no true ability to do anything as a program director. I would learn that over and over again during my nearly five years at NJ 101.5.

I signed a one-year contract for $125,000, and gave them an exclusive window to re-sign me sixty days out from the end of the one-year.

I was going to host a five-hour show Monday through Friday, and I wanted a partner—and a specific type of partner. I wanted someone older than me, someone who would not fight me for the microphone, a second banana who would never stab me in the back. Hard to find, for sure. The first guy they tried out was a producer friend of mine who didn't want to be on the air. He sounded like shit. Then they brought in Ray Rossi.

Ray was a radio journeyman. He had worked at three New York City radio stations, all under different names given him by program directors. He had never done talk. Desperate for the gig, he would go along with anything I said from the get-go. He also didn't care if or when he got to talk, and he was twenty years older than me. Not perfect, but perfect for me. I came up with the idea for the name *Jersey Guys,* just in case Ray didn't work out, so we wouldn't have to keep changing the name of the show from Carton and whoever.

We started in June 2002, and by September, we had the number-one, most-listened-to afternoon show in America. Nobody came close to dethroning us for the rest of my time there. I was nominated as talk show host of the year by *Radio & Records,* a trade publication that works in hand with the National Association of Broadcasters. I was voted one of the fifty most important talk show hosts in America by *Talkers* magazine, and even the ninth most powerful person in New

Jersey state politics. I was the king of NJ 101.5, and I loved it, other than that I wanted the same recognition in a major market. Total ego for sure, but being number one in New Jersey and the most-listened-to guy in America out of New Jersey wasn't as fulfilling ego-wise, financially, or career-wise, as if I could do it in New York or even back in Philly.

Over the years, I was approached several times to move to both markets. WMMR in Philadelphia came to me through their PD, a guy named Bill Weston. Bill had a low-rated morning show hosted by Mike Missanelli and Joe Conklin, a Philly comedian best known for his impressions of Philly athletes and icons. The show stunk because it had no energy, and the guys were always waiting for Joe to say something funny. The problem is, while Joe's great at stand-up and when he has a prepared bit, he isn't a high-energy guy. There was no way to do conversational humor, and as a result, the show was tame and boring. But I did love that it was on a rock station the rest of the day. Mike had just been fired, and they needed a real host to take over, so I met with Bill at an Applebee's on City Line Avenue, outside of Philly. The executive producer of the show was my old pal Blain Ensley. He came to lunch as well.

Things went great until Conklin showed up. He said matter-of-factly that he was the star of the show, that nobody could deliver the punch line to a joke that was his, nobody could be bluer than him. On and on and on he went. He also said I would have to change my on-air persona to work around his.

I pointed out that he was part of a dying morning show and didn't have a leg to stand on, but having been part of the successful Angelo Cataldi morning show, he thought he knew best. I called Bill the next day and declined the job. Another year in Jersey it would be.

I was approached to do mornings at WMMS in Cleveland, WDFN

sports radio in Detroit, WRKO talk radio in Boston, and eventually WFAN Radio. Along the way, I had decided that the best thing for me to do was get attention, and lots of it. If a week went by when my show wasn't being written about in some publication, that was a failed week of radio.

When Howard Stern announced that he was going to satellite radio, Rob Barnett, an executive with CBS Radio, initiated contact with me. Tim Sabean, who was running the Stern affiliate in Philly, called me about possibly replacing Stern in Philly. I still had a year to go on my contract. I wanted to do the right thing by my company, so I went to them to get permission, which my contract stated I had to do. After hemming and hawing a bit, Andy gave me a specific window in which I could talk and negotiate a contract with CBS Radio, should they offer me one.

After several meetings, it looked like I had a real chance to be one of the guys who was going to be the guy to replace Howard Stern. My last meeting was going to be with Joel Hollander, the president of CBS Radio. I went to my company one last time and described the progress. I said that before I take the Hollander meeting, I want to make sure that this is all kosher. If it's not, you have to let me save face now and not meet with Joel. Andy told me that it was all good, and that they would never stand in the way of that kind of career progress.

I met with Joel. It went great. I thought I was going to get the job. Joel was so nice, he even promised to find me an agent to represent me and make the guy cut his commission in half. I thought I was going to replace Stern. It might actually happen. Holy shit.

Sadly, though, it didn't. While I was in with Joel, the operations director of the parent company that owned NJ 101.5 sent a fax to Joel demanding a shit load of dollars to let me out of my contract.

Stabbed in the back.

I got the call from CBS on my way home from the meeting that I thought had changed my life forever. The executives wanted to know, and rightfully so, what was going on. I asked them if they would extend me a twenty-four-hour courtesy to find out and fix it, which they did. I called for a meeting with Santoro and Jim Donahoe, the douchebag who sent the fax. They didn't apologize. They also were not going to let me out of my contract.

I offered to pay the full value of my deal to get out of it. They stonewalled me, and I had no way to get out of it. They didn't care that they had robbed me of potentially replacing Howard Stern. I called both of them every bad word you could think of, and then five more. They said I was too valuable to let go. They even offered me a one-year extension for a boatload of money and equity in the company. I said no to all of it, and told them to fuck off. I would work out the contract and then plan on leaving, or worst case, hold them up for much more if I stayed.

Now I had no boss at all. I refused to speak with management ever again. Eric Johnson was soft, and anytime he tried to get involved in the show, I shut him down. He would then apologize with a bottle of wine. Not having a boss was a two-sided coin for me. Creatively it was great. I did whatever I wanted. I knew that no matter how bad the GM's reaction, Andy would always have my back. I was also producing nearly 65 percent of all the revenue for the station.

I was a rogue broadcaster. I had uncovered a planned ticket blitz of the public by state troopers, in retribution for negative media coverage of the trooper who crashed Governor Jon Corzine's car going 91 miles per hour. I had also organized more than a hundred strippers who showed up at the New Jersey State House to agitate for the repeal of the ban on smoking in bars—I called it "The 100 Stripper Rally"—and thousands of people showed up for it. But I was also number one by far, and untouchable, ratings- and revenue-wise. I was unfireable, and the only host before or after me to transcend what the station was about: traffic, weather, and nothing else. The shows were lazy and boring, and there was little pride in preparing and delivering a great show every day. It was easy to stand out. When Governor James McGreevey announced that he was a gay American and stepped down as governor, it changed the landscape of New Jersey politics and my show. I liked McGreevey a lot and always respected him. He was a lousy governor. Too many power brokers in the state knew he was gay, and always held him over a barrel because of it. McGreevey knew that I knew about his sexuality. He also knew that he needed to come on my show when there was a big statewide issue that he wanted to talk about to the most people possible. The week before he announced he was gay, he came on my show, knowing I was a "crazy out-of-control shock jock," and that I knew his secret and I could ask him anytime.

I knew because I had a dear friend who worked with Jim, and this friend told me stories about half-dressed young men in the governor's mansion at all times of the day and night, and one particular get-together at a Nets game in the governor's suite. These stories were all reported publicly well after I first heard of them and kept mum about them. McGreevey showed up and drank beer with me for an hour, and did one of the best radio spots I had ever done with a politician on the show. I felt terrible for him that he was forced into his admission, and even worse about the effect it had on him and his children.

When he stepped down, Dick Codey became acting governor. Codey, a longtime politician and crafty blue-collar, streetwise guy, seized on the opportunity to run the state. He loved being governor; the power, the game, everything. The problem for Codey was that nobody outside of the county he lived in knew him. A Quinnipiac poll had his name recognition at less than 30 percent the day he was sworn in. Codey was smart, though. He knew he needed some way to get his name out there and in a positive way. So he chose me to do it for him.

The first Wednesday of every month, our station hosted an Ask the Governor show. The news director hosted it, and the governor would come in to the station for it. The show aired after mine, and the governors arrived about thirty minutes prior, so they could hear my show before going on. I figured it was a perfect idea to do an Ask the Governor pregame show, and let callers and myself take the governor to task and make fun of him while he was trapped as a listener.

Codey came to the station one day with a plan to get attention for himself. The day before, I had done a story on how now that the Codeys were in office, they had a new platform. His wife's platform was postpartum depression. She told an emotional story about how she suffered from it after the births of their two sons. She had tried to drown them once, and contemplated putting one of her boys in the microwave once, only to be stopped by a nanny. These stories offended me as a parent. I couldn't fathom ever doing harm to my child, or to any child. It seemed to me that she was being cavalier about expressing her postpartum desire to hurt her own kids. I respect the fact that thousands of women deal with PPD, and that it is a very real issue. But my brain couldn't wrap itself around the idea that the mental demons could be so strong that a new mother would ever come close to—let alone do—the things she was describing. When I heard her comments, I vividly remember going home and looking at my two kids at the time, and being really angry that she was so comfortable talking about the idea of doing something like that. This happened on the same day that Governor Codey was blathering on about why he would never legalize medical marijuana.

I put the two together and suggested that maybe if he would legalize marijuana, women like his wife would go for a bag of Doritos as opposed to trying to microwave their kids. I added that I wouldn't be surprised if she had an underlying mental issue, which was exacerbated by the hormonal changes from having a baby. Perhaps she was crazy before she had the kids. The governor never heard the show. He heard about it thirdhand.

Codey invited along a female reporter who was right out of college and had never covered the governor or anything, for that matter. She was at the *Star-Ledger*, a paper that took shots at me every chance they could. He promised her a show and told her to make sure she documented everything that happened. As I walked out of the studio, Codey came right at me nose-to-nose with two state troopers—both armed, of course—and the young reporter flanking him. He said loud enough for all to hear, "If I was not governor, I would take you out!"

I was shocked, but I didn't back down. Still nose-to-nose, I said aloud, "What, are you kidding me? You're threatening me?"

"I would take you out," he said.

"How dare you say that? You're the governor of New Jersey!" I looked around, but nobody seemed to think his behavior was strange. He went on frothing at the mouth about how dare I say the things I said about his wife. I asked him if he had heard the show. "No, but people told me about it," he said.

"How dare you?" I moved closer, and noticed that both troopers now had their hands on their weapons. Members of his staff and the radio station separated us, and he was ushered into the studio.

If he had wanted to take me on for what I said, he was in the building early enough that he could have come on my show and attacked me. But he didn't. What he did was premeditated, and he made sure he had a reporter in his back pocket to document it for the next day's paper. He decided to start the Ask the Governor show by making a statement condemning me and what I had said, despite not having heard it firsthand.

The next day, a story appeared about how Governor Codey defended his wife's honor against the shock jock. He was an overnight sensation. I was the scourge of the earth, an out-of-control heathen who attacked a mentally unstable woman. Governor Codey was the hero on a white horse. I was the subject of TV shows, columns, and countless newspaper articles. On Mother's Day, I was the lead story above the fold for the *Star-Ledger*.

Codey wasn't done yet. Quinnipiac took a poll the day after the front-page story, and Governor Dick Codey had an approval rating of nearly 80 percent. In two weeks, he went from unknown to the most popular governor in the history of the state, thanks to me and his choreographed confrontation with me.

The state legislature then got involved. Led by Wilfredo Caraballo, they had an emergency session to vote on whether or not to censure me. About a dozen politicians met in a public forum, which I attended. At the meeting, the public could attend and ask questions. I sat in the front row to be seen, and could not believe it when a member of the public asked the politicians how many of them had heard my show that day. Not a single one said that they had heard it. Twenty minutes later, they voted to censure me. I was the first-ever private citizen to be censured by the state of New Jersey.

I was on a roll.

Codey and I had more in common than anyone thought. We were both big sports fans, and both big basketball fans. About six months later, after the incident had died down and he was running New Jersey, word got to me though a close friend that Codey wanted to make a surprise appearance on my show to bury the hatchet. Why not?

He was the most popular governor. I wasn't going anywhere, or so I thought.

Bob Ingle, the talented Gannett news chief for New Jersey, was a friend. He came on my show every Friday to dispense State House gossip. Codey went to him to set it up. The plan was that they would show up at six and spend the last hour with me on the air. I knew about it but didn't tell anyone at the station, not even Ray Rossi. The only issue was, the day that the governor was set to surprise us, I had three former terrorists in the studio talking about their time under bin Laden. As a result of their being there, four undercover FBI, CIA, and state police officers were acting as "producers," just in case. Because of this, the governor's security detail would not let him in the building until the terrorists left. Governor Codey sat outside our building for nearly forty-five minutes waiting for them to leave. When he came in, he was all smiles, and buried the hatchet with me on the air. He winked and smiled when I told him I thought that he had set the whole thing up.

Codey and I became friends that afternoon, and have supported each other's charitable causes ever since. He was one of my first callers when I got to The FAN, and I believe that if he had run for governor as opposed to Jon Corzine, he would have won in a landslide. The added result of this dustup was that I was considered the ninth most powerful person in New Jersey state politics, according to a major political poll.

"**Nappy**-headed hos": those three objectionable words changed my life. When Don Imus used that term to refer to the Rutgers women's basketball team, it shocked the entire radio universe and the country as a whole. I paid close attention, as I was interested in seeing how CBS would handle what he said. I, too, had said objectionable things over my career. Most successful talk radio guys have.

I was surprised when word came down that Imus was being fired for good. I never thought that I would get a call from CBS, based on how things had gone a year earlier during the Howard Stern fiasco. But my phone rang and it was CBS, and I was in the game. After several weeks of conversation and many cleared hurdles, I met with Mark Chernoff at Harold's Deli in Edison, New Jersey, to discuss the opening. Harold's was my spot. I had all of my big meetings there: huge sandwiches, great hospitality, and a memorable lunch.

Chernoff had approached me six months earlier about Free FM, which was CBS Radio's attempt to do FM talk. But that idea fizzled as well, due to my small-minded management cock-blocking me. That CBS would call me again was awesome and surprising. Chernoff indicated he wasn't sure if it would happen, but they had picked a guy with whom they thought I would work well, someone who would help sanitize my bad-boy image from New Jersey. He had done radio, but never on a daily basis where he was half the show.

His name was Boomer Esiason.

Chernoff gave me Boomer's number and gave mine to Boomer. The first time we ever spoke, Boomer called me. I was on my way down the shore to host my annual Jersey Guys bikini contest. I told him where I was going and he said, "Please tell me we won't be doing any of those if we get this job." I laughed and told him, "If we get the job, we won't do anything you don't want to do."

We made idle chitchat: surface stuff about family and a little bit about my life at 101.5, and that was it. We ended the call by saying that we looked forward to meeting in the near future. I went from my bikini show to a week of vacation with my family in Margate, New Jersey, a shore town next to Atlantic City. The first day of vacation, Chernoff called to ask if I was available to come into New York to do a demo show with Boomer. I said yes and planned on being in New York two days later. We would meet at Fifty-Sixth and Seventh outside the Brooklyn Diner, which was connected to the same building I worked out of when I hosted the ill-fated *Sports Guys* show nearly six years earlier. The irony didn't escape me. I liked the fact that one of my lowest career moments might be related to the site of the biggest turning point of my career.

I sat outside the diner until Chernoff showed up with a few other

CBS executives. Boomer arrived a minute or two later. We shook hands and joined the executives for the elevator ride up to the radio station. Boomer and I had never met before. We had only spoken that one time on the phone for five minutes. Chernoff told us that he and the corporate executives wanted us to do a radio show, off-air, in one of their production studios. They would throw out a topic and then Boomer and I would pretend to be doing a real show on that topic. I would drive the conversation, being the experienced radio guy, and hope that Boomer would follow along and mix it up with me.

Right before we started, Boomer told the radio executives that he wanted a minute alone with me, so he and I walked into another room. Boomer looked right at me and said, "Go for it. We have nothing to lose and everything to gain. Worst case, we both go back to our other jobs. Best case, we replace Don Imus on the legendary WFAN Radio, something that could change both our lives for the better."

We walked back into the studio. Within thirty seconds, we bantered about one topic after the next, and gave each other a hard time as if it were the most natural thing in the world. Boomer didn't flinch when I took little potshots at him, and he gave them right back. I went right at him when he would name-drop about playing with or knowing certain guys. I referred to him as a "booshie name-dropper," and he gave it right back, describing me as an unathletic sports fan who was jealous that he wasn't invited to the pro athlete dinners that he got to go to. Those dinners don't exist—he invented them on the spot, much like I was riffing on my shots at him.

We just got each other from day one. If you had walked into that room, you never would have known that we had never met, let alone never done a radio show before. What we did that day duplicates the same rapport we have on the air today. We could see and hear the executives who were sitting on a couch in the studio watching us like we were zoo animals; they were laughing and nodding their heads. We did a full hour, and when we were done, Chernoff said, "Out of all the people that tried out or were considered for the gig, that was the best we heard. Who do we have to talk to for each of you to get a deal done?"

Two months later, on September 4, 2007, the *Boomer & Carton* show began. The beginning was rough. All of the on-air hosts at the station except for Steve Somers turned their backs on us and went out of their way to discredit us and put us down. I knew we had a good show, and I thought it could be great. I also knew that as we evolved, we would sound so much younger, more vibrant, and more entertaining than all of the other shows. We just needed time and some attention.

Prior to going on the air for the first time, Boomer and I spent a few days reviewing what kind of show we would do. We met with sales and promotions and our immediate staff in preparation for September 4, 2007. We had met just about every person in the building except for one: Mike Francesa. Mike was one-half of the afternoon show *Mike and the Mad Dog*. Mike's reputation was that he was tough to work with and considered himself the de facto boss of WFAN.

I didn't like Mike. Mike didn't like me. Years earlier when I was hosting the WNEW *Sports Guys* morning show, I made a point of attacking him whenever he made a mistake on the air or lied about something he had said.

He recently told his audience that he picked the Giants to beat the Patriots in the Super Bowl and beat them big. Two days later, a listener produced an audiotape of him predicting the exact opposite before the game. I attacked and attacked and attacked. He got wind of it and wanted it to stop. How dare a fellow CBS Radio broadcaster attack him? He thought he had the clout to make me disappear.

My boss at WNEW was Jeremy Coleman. Mark Chernoff was running WFAN back then, as he does today. Mark called Jeremy and implored him to make me stop. Jeremy didn't give a shit that I was doing it, so he came to me and told me that he had been asked to make it go away. I told him that if Mike had some issue with me, he could call me himself. Jeremy relayed that info to Mark. I was told that Mike would be calling me in ten minutes at WNEW.

I went back to my office and waited for the call. I wasn't alone. The entire morning show staff came into the office. They expected a show when Mike called, and that's just what they got. The phone rang. I let it ring again and again before picking it up.

"Hello?"

"Is this Craig?"

"Yes it is. Who is this?"

"It's Mike."

"Mike who?" I figured I'd fuck with him right out of the gate.

He raised his voice. "Mike Francesa. What did you say about me on your show today?"

"Nothing."

We went back and forth cursing at each other like sailors until it was clear neither one of us was going to give any ground. I hung up on him. He never called back. Now I was getting ready to be the WFAN morning show host, and Mark asked me if I would agree to have lunch with Mike prior to our first show. It was a smart play by Mark to get us together, with the idea being for some kind of détente, and to let us know we were now on the same team. Mark thought that if Mike got to spend some time with me, man-to-man and face-to-face, Mike would be more than willing to support Boomer and me as Imus's replacement.

The lunch was set up for 11:30 at the Cup Diner in Astoria, a neighborhood place across from the radio station, which was in the heart of Queens. I met Mark at the station and we walked over to-gether. We sat down at a table and chatted a bit about the show until Mike arrived.

Mike lumbered in with a limp and a look of disgust on his face. He sat down, we ordered lunch, and then the fun began. Mike was wearing dark sunglasses. It was a beautiful August day outside. There was no need for sunglasses inside, but he never took them off. He also refused to look at me when we spoke. He would arch his head to the right and to the left, but he would never look right at me.

What he had to say was even more laughable. Mike explained how, in his opinion, our show had no chance of making it and while he could make it work, I would have no chance to make Boomer a solid radio guy every day of the week. He told me over and over how we had no chance, but that he would, if given the same opportunity. I'll never know why he wanted to make that point to me, but he made it loud and clear. The only positive thing he said was that he felt if Chernie (his nickname for Mark) felt that I was the guy, then I was the guy. He wished me good luck as he walked out of the dinner.

People always want to know whether we don't get along with the other hosts. In truth, we get along with everyone. Sadly, though, we don't interact with any of the other shows' hosts on a regular basis. We broadcast out of our own studio, which precludes us from seeing Joe and Evan, our midday show hosts, and we are long gone from the building by the time Mike Francesa gets there.

Nobody has ever done a sports show at WFAN the way Boomer and I do it, and as a result, the other hosts decided early on that since we were not doing straight sports shows like every other show on the station, we were not part of their fraternity. That never made sense to me. The better we do, the better they do. We didn't care what they thought from square one. Once we became successful, we didn't care much about them at all. Only Steve Somers was gracious to us from the day we started.

Despite the other hosts' predictions, Boomer and I wound up getting both time and attention from the listeners. One year after we began, we accomplished something that had never been done before in the history of WFAN, even with the legendary Imus hosting mornings: we were number one in every male demographic, young and old, and had become the highest-rated show on the entire station. *Boomer & Carton* had arrived—but more importantly, so had I.

A number of people have referred to me as the Howard Stern of sports radio. I must say, I don't understand why this is said as a negative. I view it as a huge compliment. Howard Stern is the greatest broadcaster in the talk radio genre, and not even arguably; he changed the format for talk radio forever. He was and is a trailblazer, and I was a big fan of his growing up. To be compared to him is better than any dopey award I could win.

Among the highlights of my five-plus years at WFAN Radio, in no particular order:

1. My first day on the air, and being able to say "*Boomer & Carton* on Sports Radio 66 WFAN."
2. Playing goalie in full hockey gear twice at Madison Square Garden for the Garden of Dreams charity, and then stopping Boomer and a bunch of legendary New York Rangers in a shootout. Of course, I found out later that the guys were aiming for me, instead of the goal. But hey, a save is a save!

3. Seeing my kids playing pickup ball with Ray Allen of the Boston Celtics, right before Boomer and I got to do the play-by-play of a legitimate NBA regular season game between the Nets and Celtics—which by itself was awesome.

4. Flying on a sponsor's private jet with Dan Marino, and trying to explain to Dan the concept of the movie *My Best Friend's Girl* (which I lent to him, and have not yet had returned). And on the same flight, Dan asking me and Boomer if there was something wrong with our producer Al Dukes: "something hereditary?"

Boomer is an interesting guy, and I've gotten to know him very well over the years. When we had been together for just a few months, we decided to throw a staff holiday party. We invited every member of our staff and their spouse or significant other. We planned the party at the downtown Manhattan Bowlmor bowling lanes. When we showed up there, we had reserved two lanes, but rather than have a laid-back, fun bowling experience, I met "Competitive Boomer" for the first time.

Most pro athletes have a competitive streak that sets them apart from mere mortals—that is, nonprofessional athletes. Boomer set us up on teams with the rule that you couldn't be on the same team as your significant other. This was a great idea. It gave everybody a chance to interact with people they might not know, or know very well.

Boomer and I captained our teams, and before we bowled the first ball, I looked in his direction and said, "A hundred dollars a game. Me versus you." We shook on it. Game on; I was pumped.

The first game went to Boomer by a healthy eighteen pins. My team beat his, though, so he was pissed. He started to read his team the riot act about paying attention and not losing focus. It was hysterical—the notion of losing a coed bowling game bothered him! I started to pick up on that, thinking I could get under his skin and distract him.

Sometimes I'm not that bright. The man played in a Super Bowl and led his team to a go-ahead score with less than two minutes left against the San Francisco 49ers. There was no way I was going to get under his skin at a bowling alley.

Shockingly, though, I took game two, and so did my team. You could see the steam coming out of Boomer's ears when the lanes went black. He ordered someone on the staff to go to the front desk and turn the lanes back on because we weren't done yet.

Boomer Esiason doesn't like a tie, and he doesn't like to lose. He kicked everyone off both lanes and told them there wouldn't be a third game. There would, however, be a me-versus-him battle to see who won head-to-head for the evening. We were tied, no money no foul, but someone had to win and it might as well be him.

We went frame by frame, and neither one of us ever led by more than a few pins until he threw a bad shot in the eighth and I had a strike. By the time I was done, Boomer needed to throw three straight strikes to beat me by one pin. Anything less than that, and I'd win. I was muttering under my breath as he started to throw his first ball, hoping to get him out of his game.

No luck—he threw a strike.

Two to go. The second ball was again—no doubt about it—a strike. I couldn't help but smile. Neither could he, but his was a stern, closed-lips type of smile.

Unless the last ball of the game was a strike, he'd lose. I was ready to jump up and down.

Boomer threw the ball down the lane with a curve like Kate Upton's hips. The ball sped down in perfectly smooth fashion and dropped all ten pins. Boomer beat me by one. Damn it, I lost!

We shook hands like men. He whispered to me, "I'm a pro athlete, and you aren't. And you aren't Joe Montana, either."

Nice to meet you, Competitive Boomer. That night started a five-plus-year battle in everything from Ping-Pong, to pool, to golf, to you-name-it.

Several times over the years, Boomer has decided to go on a diet. More than that, he has latched on to one diet fad or another, like millions of other Americans who want to lose weight. During our second year together, he signed up for a meal service that brought meals to your house. You could eat only what they gave you. One of those meals was a bland chicken and rice dish.

During that fall, I traveled with Boomer to every Monday night football game he was broadcasting from. Boomer is an excellent analyst on NFL broadcasts, and he does the games nationally on Dial Global, formerly Westwood One. While he broadcast the games, Al Dukes and I would watch it from the press box or a sponsor's VIP box. Once we were down in New Orleans for a game, and Boomer had brought his prepackaged meal with him. I happened to bump into his assistant on her way to the kitchen to heat it up.

I stopped her in her tracks and took the container to the dining hall set up for the media. Being New Orleans, there was a fresh bowl of gumbo just waiting to be eaten. I took three huge soup ladles of gumbo and poured it on top of his calorie-conscious meal. I gave it back to his assistant and then watched as she gave it to Boomer.

Boomer was in full game mode, so he didn't notice what I had done. He lapped up the entire thing in a matter of seconds.

The next morning, I asked him how his diet was going. He said he had the single best dinner he'd ever had on a diet. He went to great lengths to describe the gumbo, the sauce, and so on. Unable to contain myself, I started giggling like a schoolgirl. It wasn't long before he knew exactly what I was laughing at. It was a good thing I took pictures to show him exactly what I did. Two days later, he dropped the diet.

One of the biggest moments for any radio host is the chance to be on-air when breaking news hits. Well, on July 13, 2010, Boomer and I had our chance. We were doing our show that morning when an old friend, Erik Olesen, a VP of promotions for a major record label, came by with an up-and-coming band who had never done a North American radio interview.

The name of the band was and still is Neon Trees. They are huge now, but back then they only had one hit that they were promoting, and they had never been on the radio. We were sort of a guinea pig tryout. The thought was that if they could hang with me and Boomer, they could do any radio show. Their breakthrough hit was a song called "Animal." It was a rocking song, so our male audience was sure to enjoy a little taste of it. Plus their drummer has big boobs and is a huge Boomer fan from Cincinnati.

It was the perfect setup.

The band came in with their instruments, we fooled around with them for a bit, and then they started to play their song. The only reason a band gets up at the buttcrack to do a radio show is to let the audience hear them.

Just as the band started to play, our producer Al Dukes whispered into my ear that there was big news. It had just been confirmed that

George Steinbrenner, the eighty-year-old Yankees owner, had died. Through our talk-back button that lets me speak to him without anyone else hearing, I asked if he was sure it was 100 percent confirmed. He was.

So at that moment we needed to be talking about Steinbrenner, and not playing Neon Trees music. I waited as long as I could, but ultimately in mid-song during their first-ever radio appearance, I had to cut them off. I stopped the song and reported to New York that George Steinbrenner had died.

Millions of people tuned in to hear Boomer and me talk about his passing. If they had heard about it through the grapevine and then decided to tune in to us for details, for the first minute or so, they heard "Animal" instead. We got quite a few calls during that show.

We have a lot of fun with our callers, and I feel very territorial about them. I don't like it when people phone the radio station all day long, regardless of who is on the air. I believe that if they call us, they shouldn't call any other show, and I feel especially strong about the callers out of whom we make characters.

One of my favorite callers for about a month was a guy named Jay from Brooklyn. He had a thick Jamaican accent and lived with his mom. Anytime he tried to call in to win things from us, we wound up making him ask his mom for permission. It became a funny weekly bit. But then one day I heard him on the midday show, the afternoon show, and also on another radio station, trying to get the same bit started! We don't take his calls anymore.

My favorite caller of all time is either Joe D. from Brooklyn or Lou from Staten Island. Joe is a big-time Yankee fan. More specifically than that, he worships the memory of Joe DiMaggio and Frank Sinatra. Joe has a distinctive voice, and one that I can mimic. He also hates it when anybody makes fun of his two idols. I do both, of course. Joe once told a story about how he saw DiMaggio from a diner window, and when he made eye contact, DiMaggio nodded in his direction. This gesture made Joe think that they were friends. Hysterical!

We once invited Joe from Brooklyn into the studio and treated him like King for a Day, and he loved it. Two days later, I took a shot at DiMaggio, and Joe has never called us again. Instead he calls every other show to take shots at us. I love that guy.

Lou from Staten Island was, I figured, a young alcoholic with a major speech impediment when he drank—apparently all day, every day. We once had him convinced that Thanksgiving was in August, and that the Giants had a player named "Botchagaloop Jones," whom he even got to speak to, although it was just Al Dukes pretending to be Jones. I once bet Lou a case of Twizzlers (which he called something entirely different—he called them Tweezers) on the outcome of a game. Lou and Joe, for that matter, are real. They are not doing shtick, and they don't know that the joke is always on them. That's why they are my favorite callers.

After disappearing for nine months, Lou called us in October 2012. He sounded like a normal human being, lucid and articulate. Apparently he'd been addicted to OxyContin and some other pills. He is healthy now, which is good for him (but bad for us).

One thing that callers often ask is what Boomer is really like, and whether we are really friends. Yes, we have become very good friends, and while I am sure that he would like to spend even more time with me, I do need a break from him from time to time. Boomer promised that he would work with me until he was seventy-five, so I've got twenty-three more years to go.

In the winter of 2008, after I walked across the Brooklyn Bridge for the first time, I had a bad case of hemorrhoids—so bad that I needed a hemorrhoidectomy, which means total removal of the 'roids by a surgeon and his knife. I had the surgery the week before we flew to Arizona for the first of the two Giants-Patriots Super Bowls.

The surgery was a success, but the recovery was going to be two weeks of pure hell, according to my doctor. I laughed that off, as I have a high tolerance for pain and had endured much more serious operations. But damn if he wasn't right. It was worse than childbirth, for sure. Every uncontrollable twitch of anal muscle sent me through the roof. My body wanted to go to the bathroom, but my mind opposed the idea. I had loaded up on Vicodins to the point I had to be rivaling Brett Favre in his Vicodin heyday.

The problem was, the Vikes constipated me. I was completely backed up. The doctor instructed me to take a spoonful of laxative every twenty minutes until I finished an entire jar of it. (Normally it says not to exceed a few tablespoons a day.) I finished the jar, and nothing. No movement at all. The problem was, the next day I had to get on a plane and fly to Arizona.

I woke up at two in the morning with a strange feeling. I wasn't sure what it was, but I knew I had to get up take a shower to start my long day. I got into the shower, and then all of a sudden without warning, I exploded and released a week's worth of shit. It was up to my ankles. When I was done, it looked like a herd of donkeys had taken a dump.

I took the handheld sprayer and started to try to spray it down the drain. All of a sudden my wife came into the bathroom and said, "Holy shit, what is that?" I told her it was exactly what she just said, and went about my business. Sadly, part of that business was putting on an adult diaper.

I was also leaking the most foul-smelling ass juice any human has ever released. This was the worst recovery ever. My wife, Al Dukes, and I boarded the plane and sat in coach on the five-hour flight. I was miserable. We were packed in like sardines, and I couldn't get up—not because I wasn't allowed, but if I did, the reek coming from my diaper would have resulted in us having to make an emergency landing.

While we were at the Super Bowl broadcasting, we were fortunate enough to have our own private room, which made it easier for big-name guests to be on our show without worrying about being bombarded by producers from a hundred other radio stations who were scouting around for guests.

During one commercial break, we had about six Hall of Famers in the room milling about, as well as the coaches for the Super Bowl, Tom Coughlin and Bill Belichick. I couldn't stand up to greet any of them because it was the same deal as on the plane. Boomer knew my problem. During a moment of relative silence, he said loud enough for everyone to hear, "Hey, Craig! Be respectful and stand up and shake everyone's hands since they are kind enough to be on our show." I didn't budge, and then had to explain to six Hall of Famers and the two Super Bowl coaches that if I stood up, I would knock them out. It was a great moment, even though I have terrible flashbacks to those days. And I still owe you one, Boomer.

Boomer has a son, Gunnar, who has cystic fibrosis. Boomer started the Boomer Esiason Foundation after Gunnar was diagnosed, and has since raised over $100 million toward finding a cure. One of the most touching and lasting things Boomer has ever said to me is that he wakes up and goes to bed every day of his life with only one real goal. That goal is to try to find a way to guarantee that his son will outlive him. I signed on early to help out with the foundation in any way I could, and am proud to say that Gunnar has graduated from college. By all accounts he is doing great.

It's just after one in the afternoon on September 8, and I am sitting on the front deck of a boat I rented for my daughter's twelfth birthday party. There are forty or so friends and family members, all celebrating her birthday with us. But for this moment in time I am alone, and that's how I want it.

We have already passed the Statue of Liberty and made the left turn past Battery Park and into the East River. It's my favorite view of Manhattan. Looking north from the mouth of the river, I reflect that I have everything I could ever ask for: a great job, a couple of bucks in the bank, and a healthy family . . . and what's that looming up ahead?

It's the Brooklyn Bridge, and it's calling to me. It has always been my favorite; it's the bridge that put our show on the map for the first time, and now she's singing her siren song to me again.

Slowly we pass under the bridge. I look up, and right then and there I know it. She's got me.

I'm going to walk across her again, and it's going to be great.

Amazingly, I can't wait.

And I hope I don't forget to bring those ankle socks.

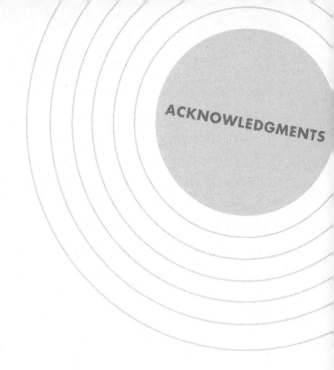

ACKNOWLEDGMENTS

"**Hey** Craig, how would you like to write a book?" Simple enough question as posed to me at Nick & Stef's restaurant in Manhattan by Ben Loehnen of Simon and Schuster. I had no idea how difficult it would be to take stories I can easily verbalize and put them down on paper in a coherent and gramatically acceptable manner.

Truth is I couldn't and wouldn't have been able to this without the guidance and support of Ben throughout the project, the amazing advice from my agent, James Dixon, who had to endure hundreds of e-mails from me throughout the process, and Leslie Wells, who agreed to edit the entire manuscript.

I went weeks without being able to put a single word down on paper and then would crank out multiple chapters in the course of a few hours.

Strangest part is, I feel like I have another book in me; there are things that I wrote that just don't fit in this book. Good things, very bad things, life-changing moments, and the Devil himself.

For now, though, I will enjoy the reality that I wrote and published a book with the greatest publishing house in America and, more importantly, that you bought it and (knock on wood) will enjoy it.

DEDICATIONS

I dedicate this book to the five most important people in my life: my wife and kids.

Kim met me, fell in love with me, and has had my back in good times and bad more than any other person on the planet. Loyal to a fault, I can say with great certainty that Kim was and is the single most important person and relationship I have ever had and without her I never would have made it as far as I did. She truly completes me and deserves everything the world has to offer and then a lot more.

Mickey J. Carton: My firstborn and the most amazingly cool and independent young woman I know. Her spirit, soul, and personality are unmatched and I truly believe she is special and destined to make the world a better place.

Sonny D. Carton: My oldest boy and such a sweet, caring kid who makes me smile every time he analyzes a situation or knows how to solve a problem quicker than I can. Smarter than his years and a much better athlete than I was at his age, he is a gift to me every day.

Lucky T. Carton: My second-oldest boy, he instantly makes me smile and lights up a room with his constant positive energy. He amazes me every day with his humor, friendship-making abilities, and cool demeanor. Nothing fazes him. He is a rock star on the field as well as off, and the world will know his name sooner than later.

Anthony I. Carton: The last of the Carton clan. Didn't see him coming but love his blossoming personality and amazing, heart-melting smile, especially when he just wakes up. Might be the smartest two-year-old on the planet. I can't wait to enjoy his life with him every step of the way.

NSB: You are the best and I can't ever thank you enough for everything you have done for me and my family.

I would also be remiss if I didn't take a moment to thank my radio family. Al Dukes, the best and quirkiest producer and man I know, who somehow gets how I think from 6 a.m. to 10 a.m. every morning; Eddie Scozzare, Bob Dwyer, and Jerry Recco for putting themselves on the line for me and with me every day; Mark Chernoff, my boss, friend, and advocate for my style of radio; and of course Boomer Esiason, who is the best partner I could ever have and who told me I am his best friend. There is no show without him—unless Phil Simms is available.

The rest of the Carton family: I wrote a lot about my family, especially as it relates to my childhood. I love all of them and thank them for the unique moments that not only made me who I am but offered great fodder for this book.